M
ys

Making Movable Wooden Toys

Alan and Gill Bridgewater

TAB BOOKS Inc.
Blue Ridge Summit, PA

FIRST EDITION
FIRST PRINTING

Copyright © 1989 by TAB BOOKS Inc.
Printed in the United States of America

Library of Congress Cataloging in Publication Data

Bridgewater, Alan.
    Making movable wooden toys / by Alan and Gill Bridgewater.

      p.   cm.
    Includes index.
    ISBN 0-8306-9179-0 ISBN 0-8306-9379-3 (pbk.)
    1. Wooden toy making. I. Bridgewater, Gill. II. Title.
III. Title: Movable wooden toys.
TT174.5.W6B728 1988
684'.08—dc19   88-7786
                                                  CIP

TAB BOOKS Inc. offers software for sale. For information and a catalog, please contact TAB Software Department, Blue Ridge Summit, PA 17294-0850.

Questions regarding the content of this book
should be addressed to:

    Reader Inquiry Branch
    TAB BOOKS Inc.
    Blue Ridge Summit, PA 17294-0214

Contents

Introduction

A smooth, polished, and painted yo-yo spinning and zinging at the end of a string; the hard clunk as a wooden ball strikes a set of turned and painted soldier skittles; pendulum toys; a pull-along truck heaped high with stenciled building blocks; spinning tops; wibble-wobble dolls; pivoted painted animals and little whittled figures—they are all wonderful!

To make a toy for a child; to carve and whittle clean-cut, sweet-smelling wood; to sit out in the sunshine with a sharp knife and block of butter-yellow lime wood; to see the crisp golden curls of wood snaking out from the lathe; and finally—after a great deal of sanding, drilling, and painting—to see the look of joy and wonder on a child's face as the toy is unwrapped—these are all part and parcel of the exciting joy-making experience of wooden toy making.

The cup-and-ball toy was very popular in late sixteenth century France. This is a detail from a contemporary print.

Three early carved wooden stump or stick dolls: (left) English seventeenth century carved oak; (middle) English stump doll seventeenth century; (right) American eighteenth century folk doll, painted with a red dress, a black cloak, and a brown bonnet.

A beautiful and characteristic nest of turned, lidded, and painted Russian dolls. Note the different costume and figure details.

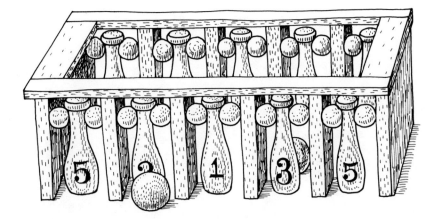

An early twentieth century American skittles game. The object is to finish up with the balls in the trap. If a ball rolls right through the gates, then the score is lost.

Welcome to a world of wooden action toys. Welcome to a world of drills, hammers, sheets of plywood, exotic hardwoods, brass pins, sticky glue, chisels, gouges, pieces of paper, pencils, and pots of paint. Okay, so you have never had much to do with woodworking and you aren't quite sure which way to hold the hammer; no matter, we will show you the way!

Not to worry if you consider yourself too old, too young, or too inexperienced—believe you me, with our carefully considered text and painstaking blow-by-blow illustrations, we will gently guide you through all the designing, making, and painting stages.

So what if you are an aged granny who has never handled a saw, or a young dad with a limited workshop, or a busy housewife, or a senior citizen, or a teacher—not to panic. Young, old, rich, or poor—this book is for you!

Not for your children a meaningless mish-mash of short-lived shop bought toys. No because we will show you how to make good, exciting, wooden working toys. What else to say, except that all the toys in this book look to a golden age when traditional toys were made with the heart as well as with the hands.

Our wooden action toys are fun. They are the kind of challenging, exciting, interesting, decorative toys that adults want to make and children want to play with.

Glossary

Acrylic—A plastic PVA type, easy-to-use, water-based, quick drying paint. Acrylics are perfect for toymaking. They can be used straight from the tube/tin; the colors are bright; they are nontoxic; and they dry so fast that several coats can be applied in the space of an hour.

Apple—A beautiful, dense-grained hardwood that carves well and takes a good polish; good for small turned toys and whittlings.

Ash—A long-grained tough wood; good for turning, but can be difficult for beginners.

Beech—A heavy, pleasant hardwood, reddish-brown in color; good for turning and for making strong toys like building blocks, balls, and push-and-pull carts.

Belly—In woodturning, just about any convex, bulging shape. Turners liken their forms to the human figure, so a turned skittle might be described as having a low belly, a narrow neck, a good solid waist, narrow shoulders, and so on.

Bird's-mouth Board—*See* V- or V-Board.

Blank—A block or slab of prepared wood. A woodturner's blank might well be disc-shaped.

Blemishes—*See* Timber Faults.

Boxwood—A dense-grained hardwood, a beautiful, butter-colored wood; good for carving and for small turned forms.

Brushes—Brushes come in a great many shapes, sizes, types and qualities. There are short-bristle heads for stenciling, flat brushes for varnishing, long-haired fine-point brushes for striping, and so on. Buy the most expensive and keep them clean. To keep the bristles in good shape, dry them well, and wrap the head in thin plastic film.

Calipers—A two-legged drawing/measuring instrument used for stepping off measurements. Woodturners use curve-legged calipers to measure inside and outside diameters.

Centers—The pivotal points at either end of the lathe. At the left-hand end, the pronged drive center, is a push-fit in the spindle, which in turn is carried in the headstock. At the right-hand end, the dead center, is a tapered push-fit in the tailstock casting. In *prong chuck*, or *between center* work, the wood is pivoted between the two center points.

Centering—Assuming the wood is square, the ends are first of all marked off with diagonals and inscribed with circles. Tangents are marked to the circles to produce octagons and the waste corners along the length of the work are removed with a drawknife, plane, or rasp. With the work ready for mounting on the lathe, the wood is tapped onto the pronged drive center, the tailstock is brought up towards the work and clamped into position, the dead center is wound up and driven into the wood, and finally the tool rest is fixed so that it is just clear of the work. With the tool grasped in both hands and steadied on the tool rest, the initial cylinder is roughed out.

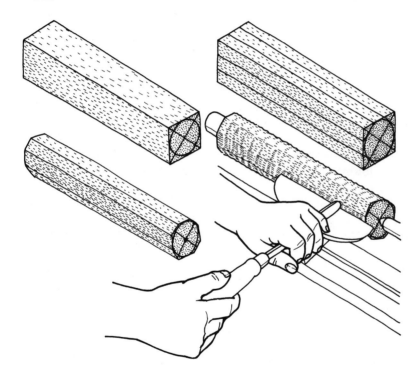

Centering and Roughing out. Set out diagonals, inscribe circles, mark out octagons and clear away the waste - secure the wood between lathe centers and swiftly cut the wood down to a cylinder.

Center Punch—A small steel spike used for marking centers prior to lathe centering.

Cherry—A beautiful, close-grained, red-brown hardwood that is good for carving and turning.

Chuck—Any type of wood-holding device used on the lathe. There are three-/and four-jaw chucks, chucks with spigots, pins, collars and collets, woodscrew chucks, cup chucks, wooden chucks, and so on. It is best to

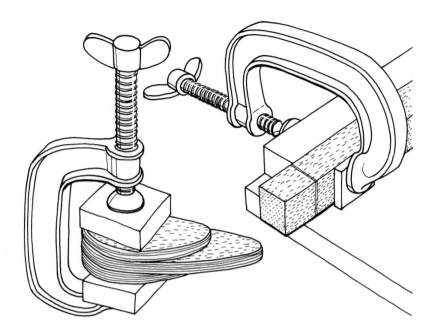

Clamps/Cramps. Using clamps to hold and secure the wood while it is being worked; (left) holding the work until the glue is dry; (right) holding the wood while it is being sawn.

make do with the pronged and screw chuck, and then to buy specific types as you become more experienced and as the need arises.

Clamps, Cramps, and Holdfasts—Screw devices used for holding wood while it is being worked or accurately cut. They are variously called G-clamps, C-clamps, strap clamps, and so on. In use, the wood to be screwed, glued, or cut is protected with off-cut wasters.

Compass—A two-legged instrument used for drawing circles and arcs. Best to get a long-legged, multipurpose, screw-operated type.

Contact Adhesive—An easy-to-use, low-stress adhesive. In use, it is smeared on both surfaces, then after ten minutes or so the surfaces are brought together.

Coping Saw—A fine-bladed frame saw used for fretting out thin section wood. A good saw for toymakers because the blade can be quickly removed and refitted, it's the perfect saw for cutting out holes and for working tight corners and curves.

Craft Knife—Just about any sharp knife that might be used for cutting paper, cardboard, wood, and string. It is best to have one with a short, fixed, easy-to-change blade.

Cup Chuck—A specific wood-holding lathe chuck, used to hold cylinders and spigots. The inside diameter of such a chuck is usually about 2 inches.

Cut-In—In wood turning, the act of sliding the parting tool or the skew chisel deep into the wood. Also, the act of making an initial cut.

Designing—Working out forms and details by visiting museums, looking around craft shops, making drawings, and constructing prototypes. We usually gather up all our research material, make models with bits of card and string, and then draw up measured designs.

Drawknife—A traditional easy-to-use, two-handled knife used for cutting and carving free forms. The work is best supported in a clamp or vise, with the tool being drawn along the work towards the user. A good tool for cutting away the waste prior to between-center wood turning.

Drafting Paper—*See* Tracing Paper.

Drilling Holes—Best to work with a small, easy-to-use, silent-running, hand-operated, breast drill. In use, support the work with a waster, check the angle of the drill with a set square, and secure the wood with a clamp. Hold and steady the drill with one hand, and set it in motion with the other hand.

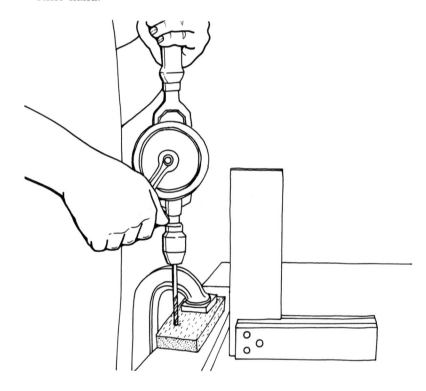

Drilling. Protect the bench and the work with scraps of wood. Use a square to make sure that the drill is at 90° to the work.

Enamel Paints—Gloss-finish oil-based paints, paints that are described as being nontoxic. In toy making, it is most important that your chosen paints conform to *toy safety* standards. If in doubt, use paints described as being suitable for model and toy making, or use acrylic paints.

Exotic—In the context of this book, a wood that originates in another country, and/or has special, beautiful, unusual or attractive qualities. One man's ordinary piece of rosewood might be another man's exotic wood!

Faceplate—In wood turning, a perforated circular metal plate that is attached to the headstock of the lathe, on which the work is mounted. The faceplate is screwed onto the drive mandrel and screws are fixed through the faceplate and into the work.

Felt-tip Pens—Ordinary water or spirit-based felt-nibbed pens. Wood can be color stained with felt tips and then varnished.

Files—Files come in all shapes and sizes, everything from small needle and riffler files to large two-handed rasps. Toy makers need a good selection.

Filler—Used to fill breaks, cavities, and scratches. It is best to use a stable two-tube plastic/resin filler that can be sanded, sawn, and drilled.

Finishing—The process of filing, sanding, rubbing down, staining, painting, varnishing, and otherwise bringing the work to a satisfactory structural, textural, and visual conclusion.

Fit-and-Fix—To bring the work to good order by rubbing down, fitting, gluing, and putting together with screws and/or bolts.

Fretsaws—Fretsaws belong to the same family as piercing and coping saws. They have G frames and flexible, easily removable blades. A good saw for cutting holes and curves in thin-section plywood. In use, the frame is guided and steadied with one hand while the handle is pushed and maneuvered with the other. *See* Coping Saw.

Friction Fit—To fit together two or more parts so that one part is a perfect fit within another. If you have made your own wooden chuck, the wood to be turned needs to be a good, tight, secure friction fit.

G-clamps or C-clamps—*See* Clamps, Cramps, and Holdfasts.

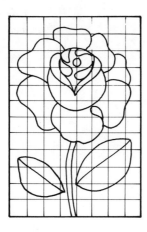 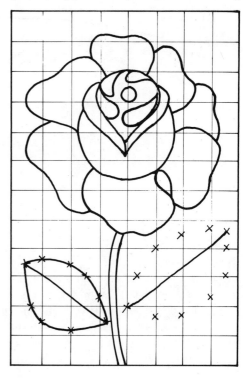

Enlarging gridded patterns and designs. Draw a grid to the required size and transfer the design one grid square at a time.

Gridded Working Drawing—In the context of this book, a drawing or illustration that has been drawn on a scaled grid. If, for example, the scale of the grid is described as being *four grid squares to 1 inch*, then the grid squares can be read off as ¼-inch units of measurement. If you want to change the scale, all you do is draw up a larger grid and transfer the image one square at a time. When you come to reading a grid, it is best to set your calipers to the suggested inch scale and then use the calipers to read off and to establish sizes.

Hammers and Hammering—Best to use either a 4-ounce ball-peen or a cross-peen hammer. Hold the hammer well towards the end of the handle, use small brass or steel pins, make sure the pins are staggered or off set, and see to it that they are punched below the surface. *Note*: If, in toy making, you can choose between screws or nails, go for small brass screws.

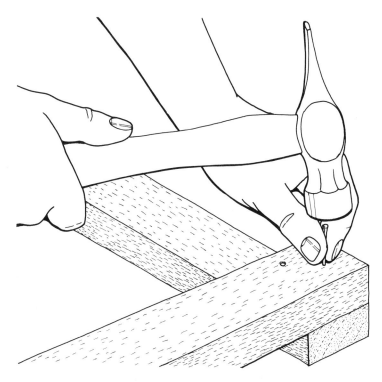

Hammer. Hold the hammer well towards the end of the handle. Note the use of small offset pins.

Hand Drill—*See* Drilling Holes.

Headstock—In wood turning, the mass of metal at the left-hand end of the lathe. The headstock carries two trust bearings in which the spindle or mandrel revolves. The power is supplied to the spindle by means of an electric motor and a drive belt. The spindle has an external screw for chucks and faceplates, and an internal taper for the pronged center.

Holly—A beautiful cream-colored, close-grained wood; an easy-to-work wood that turns well and takes fine details.

Inspirational Designs/Materials—In the context of this book, this term might refer to: toys that you have seen in museums and shops; manufacturer's literature; old books; our designs; magazine clippings; and so on. It's a good idea to keep a sketchbook/scrapbook and to take note of interesting designs, motifs, patterns, and fixings.

Lathe—In wood turning, a wooden or metal frame called a bed, a headstock and tailstock, an electric motor, a tool rest, and various fittings and fixtures; (a) headstock; (b) spindle or drive center and mandrel; (c) tool rest; (d) tailstock center; (e) tailstock; (f) tailstock wind-up handle or center advance; (g) lathe bed; (h) quick action clamp for the tool rest; (i) adjustment nut for tailstock; (j) distance between centers.

Lathe Safety. Pre-Switch-on Checklist

1. Always make sure that faceplate work is well mounted and secure.
2. Before you switch on the lathe, turn the work over by hand and make sure that it is clear of the tool rest.

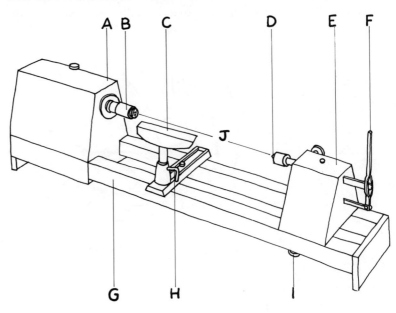

Lathe. (A) headstock (B) spindle or drive center (C) tool rest or T-rest (D) tailstock center (E) tailstock (F) spindle advance, bar, or wheel (G) bed (H) quick-action clamp for the rest (I) clamp nut for the tailstock (J) "between centers"

3. Tie back your hair, roll up your sleeves, and generally make sure that you aren't going to get dragged into the lathe.
4. Do not touch the pulleys, belts, or the work while the lathe is running.
5. Never leave children alone with the lathe.
6. Stop the motor before testing with a template or with calipers.
7. Move the rest well out of the way before sanding.
8. When polishing, do not wrap the cloth around your fingers.
9. Wear safety glasses.
10. Make sure that your chosen wood isn't dust-toxic.
11. Hold all the tools firmly.

12. Make sure that the cut-out switch is within easy reach.
13. Make sure that the tools are in good order with no loose or split handles.
14. Never ever reach over the lathe while it is running.

Lime—A knot-free easy-to-work wood; a good wood for turning, shaping, and carving; a good wood for beginners.

Maple—Easy-to-work; good for turning.

Maquette—A small working model or prototype made prior to using the best materials. Maquettes might be made from cardboard, Plasticine, modeling clay, or just about any inexpensive material that comes to hand.

Masking Tape—Also called *drafting tape*; a sticky contact tape, it might be used when painting for masking areas that you don't want painted, for strapping up glued wood, for securing drawings, and so on. A good item to have in the workshop.

Master Design—The final measured working drawing; the drawing from which all the details are taken.

Modifying—The process of changing and generally redesigning part or parcel of the project to suit your own needs.

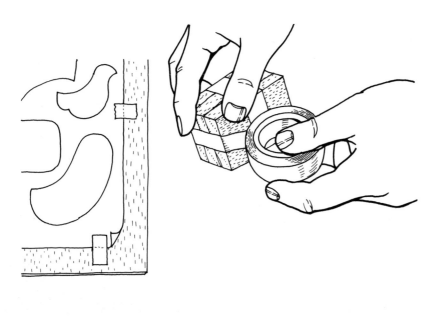

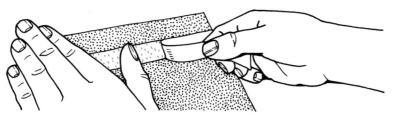

Masking tape. Might be used for holding tracing paper down on the board, for clamping small objects that have been glued, and for masking off areas during painting.

Muffled Vise—If you are working on a spherical, curved, or delicate piece of wood and it needs to be held in the vise, then the jaws of the vise should be covered with a soft material like sponge, rubber, felt, or old rags.

Multi-Chuck—A multipurpose lathe chuck. Although such chucks are very expensive, they do simplify many, otherwise difficult, turning operations.

Naive Art/Design— Any primitive, unsophisticated, uninhibited, traditional, innocent, self-taught, folk-art design or piece of art work.

Off-Cuts—Bits and pieces of scrap wood left over from projects. They are best saved for small jobs and for making prototypes.

Painting and Painting Area—When you come to painting, start by making sure that the object to be painted and the area in which you are going to do the painting are both clean, dry, and free from dust. To this end, it's best to work in an area outside the main wood workshop, say a corner of a spare bedroom or perhaps another shed out in the garden.

Spend time carefully setting out all your paints and materials, and generally see to it that all your brushes, tubs, water containers, and cloths are close to hand.

The objects to be painted need to be supported while they are wet. They can be hung on a line, placed on a wire rack, hung from wire hooks, and so on. Think this step out before you start painting.

The order of work will, of course, depend on your chosen paint and the object to be painted, but generally the wood needs to be primed, undercoated, top coated, decorated and detailed, and varnished.

Most of the projects favor the use of acrylics rather than oil-based paints, because the former kind of paint is so easy to use. There are pros and cons for both kinds of paint; on the one hand acrylics dry very quickly, the brushes can be washed in water, and the colors are bright; but on the other hand, although gloss enamels do take up to 24 hours to dry out and the brushes do need to be cleaned in spirit, the colors have a special full-bodied quality. If you are a beginner, it is best to start with acrylics, then to experiment with various paint types. *Warning: In the context of toymaking, it's vital that your chosen paints be nontoxic; the paints should conform to the "Toy Safety Act" standards. If in doubt, talk to your supplier.*

Parana Pine—A good, straight-grained, knot-free wood; good for carving, jointing, and turning.

Parting Tool—A wood turning tool used for parting off the waste at either end of the work, or for turning details where a narrow cut is needed.

Pencils and Pencil-Press Transferring—It is best to use a soft 2B pencil for designing and tracing, and a hard "H" for pencil-press transferring. When you want to transfer some part of the master design through to the working face of the wood, take a tracing, line-in the back of the design with a 2B pencil, tape the tracing to the wood, and then go over the drawn lines with a hard pencil. Never cut the master designs up and always keep the tracings.

Penknife—Just about any small bladed fold-up clasp knife.

Piercing Saw—A small frame saw, sometimes called a jeweler's saw, very much like a coping or fret saw. Good for small tight curves and corners.

Pivot—A point, rod, shaft, or dowel on which another part swings, turns, or rolls.

Plug Cutter—A drill-like tool that bores out short dowels or plugs of wood. Plug cutters are designed so that the resultant plugs exactly match up with standard drill sizes.

Plum—A really beautiful, easy-to-work wood. Streaky, warm-brown in color, it is a good wood for turning, shaping, and carving. If you are cutting down an old plum tree, don't burn it; use it on the lathe or for whittling.

Plywood or Multi-ply—When you are making toys with plywood, always use a close-grained, white, smooth-faced, best-quality type; such a wood is made up from layers that are about $\frac{1}{16}$ inch thick. In use, multi-ply can easily be cut and worked with all faces and edges being smooth and even. Do not use coarse centered plywood known as *stout heart, block ply,* or *thick center,* because the wood is so soft and coarse that it's almost impossible to rub down or to take to a good, smooth, dense finish.

Prepared Wood—A wood that has been planed and cut to a standard size. *Note*: Sizes differ from country to country.

Profiles—In the context of this book, any cut-out, cross-section, drawn shape, or flat fretted form.

Prototype—A working model made prior to the project. If you have doubts as to whether or not the project will work, or if you are making modifications, then it is best to iron out all the wrinkles by making a mock-up, dummy, or prototype.

PVA Glue—Although there are many glues and adhesives to choose from— all with varying qualities and usages—in the context of this book, we recommend the use of PVA glue or polyvinyl acetate. PVA is usually packaged in an easy-to-use container. It's ready to use, it doesn't have to be stirred or mixed with water, it has a long shelf life, and spills can be wiped up with a wet cloth. *Note*: PVA glue isn't suitable for toys that are going to be left out in damp conditions.

Resin Glue—A two-tube resin-to-hardner adhesive; a good glue that needs to be used with care. Always read instructions.

Rosewood—A good wood for turning; decorative and durable, but a bit difficult to work.

Rough Out—To chop or cut away the waste. In wood turning, the square section wood is quickly roughed out and then turned down to a cylinder.

Rubbing Down—Working through the graded sandpapers and sanding the wood down to a smooth finish. Rubbing down is messy, it's best done out of doors and well away from the painting area.

Saws and Sawing—Although we do use many saw types—everything from a tenon and gents to coping, fret, and piercing saws—you can make do with just two saws, a tenon saw and a coping saw. Don't make do with a "handed-down" antique; it is much better to buy the best tools that you can afford, and to look after them. In use, support and steady the wood with one hand, and push, guide and maneuver with the other hand. Start by steadying the blade with the thumb and by making three or four pull strokes.

Sawtooth or Forstner Drill Bit—A bit with a small center point; a bit that bores a cleanly finished flat-based hole.

Scalpel—A fine-bladed, razor-sharp craft knife, used for tidying up small details, and for cutting cardboard and paper.

Scraper—A woodturning tool that scrapes, rather than cuts, the spinning wood.

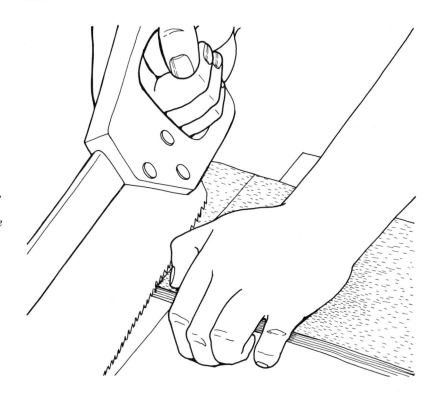

Sawing. To start sawing, draw the blade upwards several times on the edge of the wood to cut a small notch. Use your thumb knuckle to steady and position the blade.

Set Square—Also called a *try square*. If you want to test your work for straightness or for 90-degree angles, then you need a square. It is best to get one with a wooden stock and a metal blade.

Sharpening Tools—Your chisels, gouges, and knives must be kept sharp. To this end, you need an oilstone. When you come to sharpening, dribble a little light-oil onto the stone. For chisels, place the blade on the stone with the back edge of the bevel slightly raised at an angle of about 5 degrees, keep your hand steady and move the blade backwards and forwards. When you come to sharpening your knife, again hold the blade at 5 degrees to the stone, only this time you need to work both sides of the blade.

Skew Chisel—A wood turning chisel with the edge inclined at an angle of about 70 degrees to the side. It is ground on both sides and is used as a cutting tool; good for turning soft woods where a scraping action would rip the fibers.

Skittle Turning—Any small-shaped doll-like spindle that has been turned between centers.

Spigot—A narrowing at the end of a turning. For example, a 2-inch-diameter cylinder, stepped and reduced to 1 inch.

Spigot Chuck—A lathe chuck designed to grip and hold a spigot. Made of metal or wood, the chuck is so shaped that it will grip one end of a piece of work without the need for the work to be supported by the tailstock.

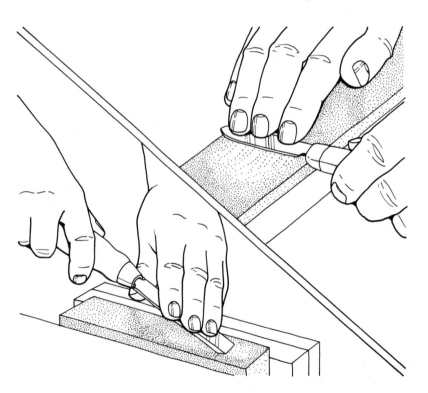

Sharpening chisels and knives; (left) hold the blade at 5° to the stone and rub down the bevel; (right) hold the knife blade at 5° and work both sides of the blade.

Spindle Gouge—A lathe tool, a gouge with a deep half-circle C section; a good multipurpose tool that can be used for roughing out and shaping.

Stencils and Stenciling—The art and craft of applying a painted design, motif or pattern by cutting *windows* in thin plastic, cardboard or paper, and then brushing or spraying paint through the holes and onto the surface to be decorated. In the context of this book, we favor using clear plastic, contact film, as used by graphic designers.

Stick Tools—Variously shaped and sectioned sticks, rods, and dowels that can be used for supporting sandpaper. Such sticks are best collected or found.

Straight Saw—A straight-bladed, fine-toothed wood-working saw.

Sycamore—A good wood for toymaking; a light-colored hardwood, smooth-grained, easy to work; a wood with low smell/taint characteristics. It is good for toys that might be sucked by babies.

Tailstock—The right-hand end of the lathe; the casting that carries the dead center. *See* Lathe and Centering.

Timber Faults—If wood is cracked, split, stained, warped, twisted, knotty, full of woodworm holes, or whatever, then it is faulted and not suitable for toy making: (a) splits called cup shakes; (b)off-center vertical cuts resulting in uneven grain spacing; (c) bits of bark and such that grow into the tree resulting in flawed wood; (d) sudden drying causes medular splits that go right through to the heartwood (bad for wood turning); (e) heartwood can be difficult to work; (f) dead branch roots result in dead knots; (g) a hole left by a dead knot; (h) warping, planks warp in the opposite direction to the end grain.

Tool Rest—A T-shaped casting that is mounted between lathe centers and designed so that it can slide into position and be fixed at center height. In use, the rest is secured as close as possible to the wood being turned. The rest acts as a fulcrum for the tools.

Tracing Paper—Might also be called drafting paper; a strong see-through paper. In use, a tracing is taken from the master design, the back of the tracing is lined in with a soft pencil, and finally a hard pencil is used to pencil-press transfer the traced lines through to the working side of the wood.

Trundle Toy—Any large-wheeled push-and-pull toy.

Turning—Working a round-section object on a lathe. *See* Lathe.

Undercoat—A flat coat of paint applied after the primer and before the top coat. For a top-quality finish, the work ought to be primed, have two undercoats, a topcoat, be detailed and decorated, and finally be varnished.

Varnish—For the projects in this book, it is best to use a clear/golden, high-gloss yacht varnish.

V- or Vee Board—Also called a V-table, a fretsaw board, and a bird's-mouth fret table. In use, the board is clamped to the workbench so that the V-notch extends beyond the surface. The sawing is done as near as possible to the vertex of the V.

V-section Tool—Any woodworking gouge that cuts a V-section trench.

Vise—A bench-mounted screw clamp, used for holding and securing wood while it is being worked.

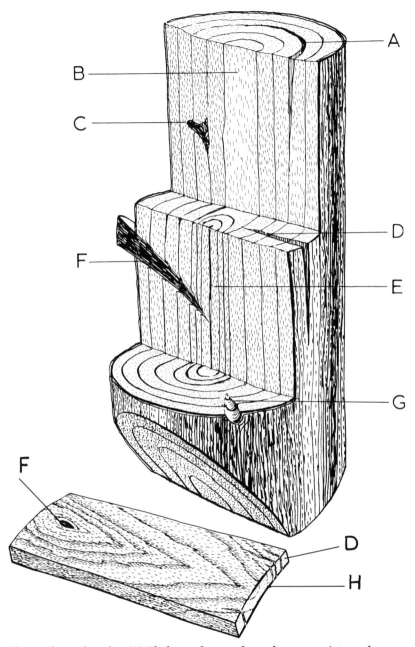

Timber and wood faults. (A) Shakes, splitting along the curve of annual growth rings. (B) Wood cut near the outside of the tree has an uneven grain. (C) Internal faults, usually caused by damage during the life of the tree. (D) Splitting caused by too rapid drying. Wood must be seasoned slowly. (E) Heart wood. (F) A knot, the root of the branch. (G) Knot falling out, leaving a scar. (H) Warping, planks warp in the opposite way to the end grain.

Wax—Wax used to finish, polish, or burnish wood. It is best to use a clear beeswax.

Wasting—Sawing, turning, gouging, or otherwise cutting away the waste.

Whittling—From the old Saxon word *thwitan*, meaning to cut and pare wood with a knife. The word has come to mean small spontaneous carvings like love tokens, paper knives, ball-in-a-cage puzzles, and linked chains.

Woodscrew Chuck—A lathe chuck used for small work. The chuck is mounted on the mandrel and the work is screwed onto the chuck's single central woodscrew.

Wood-turning Tools—Although the term can be used for all the gouges, chisels, scrapers, centers, chucks, faceplates, and calipers that might be used in woodturning, it is generally taken to mean the cutting gouges, chisels, and the scrapers.

Workbench—In toy making, a table out in the garage, an old kitchen table in a spare room, or a woodworker's bench complete with a vise. The bench needs to be strong and stable.

Working Drawings—All the sketches, designs, and notes that lead up to a scaled and measured drawing.

Working Face—The best side of the wood; the side that shows; the important face.

Work-out Paper—Rough paper on which all the preproject notes, details, and sketches are worked out. It is best to have a hardcover sketchbook.

Making a
Yo-Yo

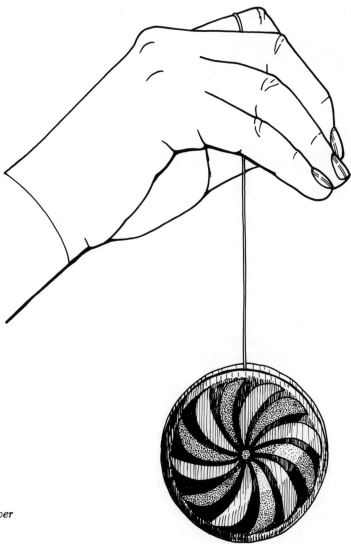

*Fig. 1-1. In use, the cord is looped over
a finger. The object is to wind and
unwind the yo-yo on its string.*

KNOWN IN EIGHTEENTH CENTURY ENGLAND AS A *QUIZ*, IN FRANCE AS A *BAND-alore*, and variously over the centuries as an *emigrette*, a *Prince of Wales' Toy* and even in Japan as an *eleyo*, the yo-yo must surely be one of the all-time favorite action toys. The yo-yo was, I clearly remember, one of my first playthings. In the late 1950s, as a lad of about ten, I impatiently saved up my pennies for many weeks so that I could buy an "amazing new American wonder toy." I neither knew nor cared that, far from being new or American, or as one Persian newspaper reported, "new, dangerous, time-wasting, immoral, and American," the yo-yo craze was in fact a rerun of similar yo-yo epidemics that had, by way of China and Persia, swept across England, Europe, and America in the 1930s, the 1850s, and the 1790s. About the only thing that I knew for sure in those far away childhood days was that my splendid, bright red, deeply-slotted toy, my smooth plastic "Guaranteed Genuine Yo-Yo" was beautiful, and I was fast becoming one of the best yo-yo players in my class. As to exactly how many yo-yo's were made and sold in the fifties, the figure is reckoned to be in excess of 100 million.

In use, the cord is looped over the index finger of the right hand and the yo-yo, best if it's made of turned wood, is dropped and unwound. As it comes to the end of its cord, it is jerked upwards, with the effect that the impetus of the spinning wheel returns it to the hand (FIG. 1-1). The whole art of using the yo-yo is not so much getting it to go up and down, although this is tricky enough, but rather seeing how long it can be kept in motion and for tricks. A yo-yo is indestructible, without batteries, springs or micro chips, a wonderful action toy!

CONSIDERING THE PROJECT

The yo-yo is, at one and the same time, one of the most basic and one of the most difficult projects in this book. This is not to say that the making stages are particulary complex—the main shape can easily be roughed out in about ten minutes. It's just that the success window that decides whether or not a yo-yo is actually going to work is pretty small. This being so, be warned; the success of a yo-yo hinges on the two words *balance* and *finish*. If you enjoy working on projects that are small, tight, and precise, and if you are a painstakingly patient worker, then it could be that this project is for you.

Have a look at the inspirational designs and working drawings. At a grid scale of four squares to 1 inch, the yo-yo is about 2½ inches in diameter and 1¼ inches wide (FIGS.1-2 and 1-3). Note how the wood is held and worked between centers, and how the profiles are measured and achieved by using a small cardboard template. See also that, in terms of time, material, and success, it is a good idea to make at least two yo-yos at a time. If you go to the trouble of preparing the wood and setting up the lathe, then it's as easy to make two forms as it is to make one.

This way, if you are lucky, you will get two toys for the price of one. If worst comes to worst and you make a mess of one yo-yo, then the other

Fig. 1-2. Painting designs. The scale is four grid squares to 1 inch.

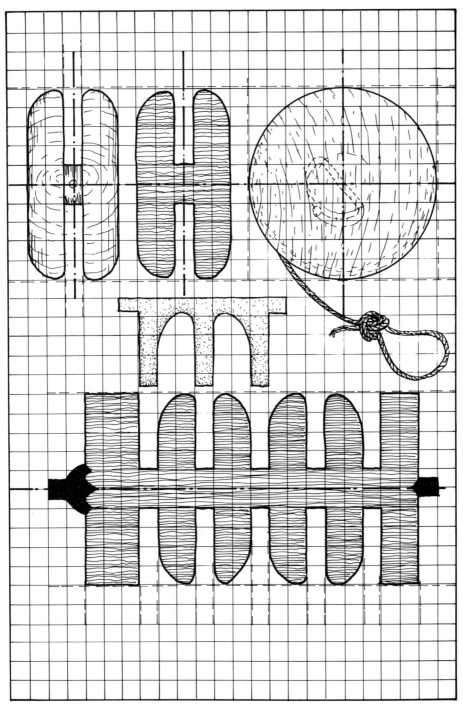

Fig. 1-3. Working drawing. The scale is four grid squares to 1 inch. Note the ¼-inch and ½-inch spacings and the use of a template.

one will work out. Of course it's not only a case of spreading the risk, it's also much easier to maneuver the tools when you are working on a longer piece of wood.

Bearing in mind that the yo-yo needs to be hand-sized and precisely symmetrically balanced, select a dense, easy-to-work, knot-free, tight-grained wood like holly, beech, or box.

TOOLS AND MATERIALS

You need ✦ A piece of attractive, easy-to-turn, dense wood at about 2¾ inches square and 5 to 6 inches long. You could use holly, beech, box, ebony, or even lignum vitae ✦ Workout paper ✦ Tracing or drafting paper ✦ Strong thin cardboard or thin plywood sheet ✦ A pencil and measure ✦ A pair of compasses ✦ A pair of scissors ✦ A craft knife or scalpel ✦ A plane or drawknife ✦ A center punch ✦ A small wood-turning lathe ✦ A selection of wood-turning tools, including a ¼-inch-thick parting chisel ✦ A pair of calipers ✦ The use of a workbench and vise ✦ A small, straight saw ✦ About 6 inches of very thin fuse-type wire ✦ A pack of graded sandpapers ✦ A selection of stick tools—you might use anything from a lolly stick to the edge of an old ruler ✦ A hand drill with a ⅛-inch-diameter drill bit ✦ About 40 inches of strong cord, best if it is smooth and silky ✦ A selection of acrylic paints ✦ A tin of yacht varnish ✦ A selection of broad- and fine-point soft-haired artist's brushes

ESTABLISHING THE DESIGNS
AND CUTTING THE TEMPLATES

Have a look at the working drawings and sections. Note the overall diameter of 2½ inches, the width of 1¼ inches, the ¼-inch-wide cord slot, the simple round-ended profile, and the ½-inch-diameter central core (FIG. 1-3). Decide just how you want your yo-yo to be, then draw the designs to size. When you have what you consider is a good workable cross-section profile, take a piece of tracing paper and a soft pencil and make a crisp firm-lined tracing. This done, turn the tracing paper over so that the penciled side is face down, then use a hard pencil to press-transfer the traced lines through to the working face of your piece of template card.

Now with the scissors and the craft knife, carefully cut out the little three-pronged template form. Finally, take the template and check its symmetry by drawing around it with a sharp pencil. If all is correct, you should be able to place the template faceup or facedown and still be able to achieve a perfectly balanced image (FIG. 1-4).

TURNING OFF THE CYLINDER AND FIRST CUTS

Take your carefully selected 2¾-inch-square, 6-inch-long piece of wood and, assuming that the ends have been cut square, use a pencil and ruler to mark

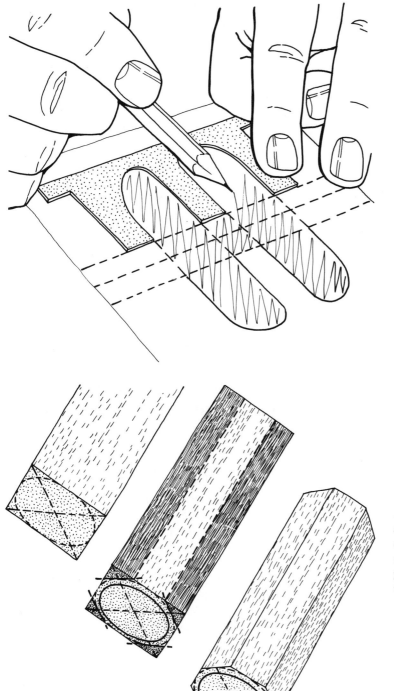

Fig. 1-4. Establish the shape and size of the yo-yo and cut the template.

Fig. 1-5. First cuts. Mark the square-cut wood with diagonals, inscribe circles to establish the waste, use a plane, rasp, or drawknife to remove the waste.

off diagonals. Now take your compass, set it at a radius of 1¼ inches, and mark off on each end of the wood a 2½-inch-diameter circle. This done, use a pencil and straightedge to mark off tangents to the circles—tangents that cross the diagonals at right angles to produce an octagon. Shade in the resultant end-of-wood octagons and link them by running lines from their corners down the length of the wood (FIG. 1-5).

Now, with either a plane, rasp, drawknife, chisel, or the tool of your choice, clear away the bulk of the corner waste. Punch in the center marks at both ends of the wood and set the wood securely between lathe centers. Once you have made sure that the drive-center prong is well into the wood, and this might require that you give the wood a tap with a mallet, place the T-rest into position and set it as close as possible to the work and a little below the centerline.

Check that all is correct, switch on the lathe, and start the turning process by using a round-nosed chisel to clear away the rough. With the tool held at a slight oblique dragging angle, work backwards and forwards along the spinning wood. Continue to work a steady and even traverse until the unevenness is removed and you have achieved a true cylinder.

With the calipers set at a distance of 2½ inches, take the ¼-inch parting tool and make three or four pilot cuts along the length of the wood. When the depth of these cuts is at a finished cylinder size of 2½ inches diameter, verify it with the calipers, then take either a square or an oblique chisel and turn off the waste until the work is down to the level of the pilot cuts.

CUTTING THE SLOTS AND THE PROFILE

Once you have turned off the 2½-inch diameter cylinder, take the pencil and ruler and, starting about ½ inch or so in from the drive end of the wood, mark off the various slots and profiles that go to make the two yo-yos. From left to right, mark off the nine divisions in the order ¼ inch, ½ inch, ¼ inch, ½ inch, and so on, until you have five ¼ inches alternating with four ½ inches. When you are absolutely sure that the divisions are correct, take the ¼-inch-wide parting tool and, starting with the first ¼-inch-wide mark, drive the tool into the wood to a depth of exactly 1 inch. Do this at all five of the ¼-inch-wide divisions to leave ½-inch-wide projections and ½-inch diameter central core (FIG. 1-6).

The next bit is tricky. With the template and your chosen tool (best to use a skew chisel), cautiously round off the ends of the ½-inch-wide projections and gradually work toward the desired yo-yo template shape. With a sliding, rolling, and shaving cut, work backwards and forwards, and from shoulder to shoulder until the template is a perfect fit (FIG. 1-7). With the cutting edge held at a flat angle to the work, cut from the shoulders down into the ¼-inch-wide slot. Repeat this sliding and cutting action to obtain the required shape. When you have completed one side of the shoulder, work the other shoulder in like manner, only this time cut in the opposite direction.

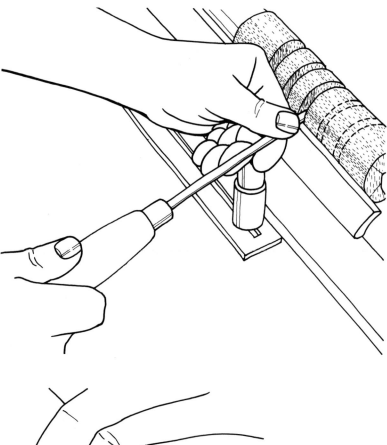

Fig. 1-6. Cutting the slots and the profile. Drive the ¼-inch-wide parting tool into the wood to a depth of exactly 1 inch.

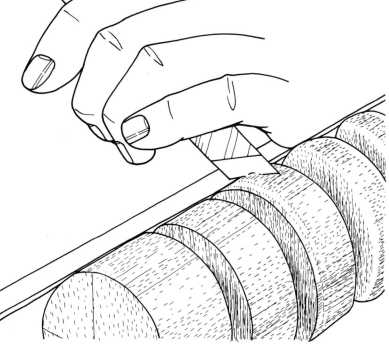

Fig. 1-7. Cutting the slots and the profile. Work down from the shoulder, with a sliding, rolling, shaving cut, until the template is a good fit.

When you have checked the form with the template and by eye, take strips of graded sandpaper and cut the surface back to a smooth finish. Finally, when you consider the work well turned and finished, remove it from the lathe. Secure the straight saw teeth-up in the jaws of the vise and separate the two yo-yos by running the work back and forth across the teeth.

FINISHING, CORD-FIXING, AND PAINTING

With the yo-yo well secured in the jaws of a cloth-muffled vise, use the hand drill and the ⅛-inch-diameter drill bit to drill a single clean hole through the central core. Carefully twist the fuse wire around one end of the yarn, then thread the yarn through the core and remove the fuse wire and fix with a sliding knot (FIG. 1-8). Stand with your arm outstretched holding the yo-yo string and, with the yo-yo just touching the floor, cut the string to length and tie a nonslip finger loop. Now, wind the string around the yo-yo clockwise or counterclockwise, it makes no matter, and have a tryout.

The yo-yo will probably fall with a shudder, and when it comes to rest at the bottom of its cord it will have an off-balance tilt. Identify the heavy side, then support the yo-yo on a wad of rags and rub down the offending face with the sandpaper. And so you continue rubbing down one side, having a trial go, rubbing down the other side, having a trial go, and so on, until you have achieved, as near as possible, perfect balance. There is no easy shortcut to balance the yo-yo other than by slow trial and error, so be patient.

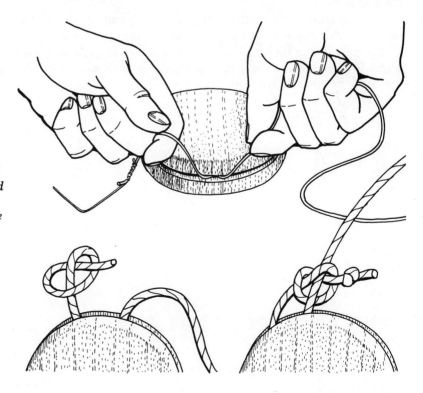

Fig. 1-8. Finishing, cord fixing, and painting. Thread the fuse wire around one end of the yarn, thread the yarn through the core and remove the wire, secure the cord with a sliding knot.

When you have made a good smooth-running well-balanced toy, then clear away all the debris, make sure that the yo-yo is free from dust, and then retreat to your clean, dust-free painting area. Take a little thinned varnish and a clean brush and, being careful not to get any varnish on the cord, lay on a swift coat. When the varnish is dry, take the finest grade glasspaper or flourpaper and give the yo-yo a swift rubbing over, just enough to remove bumps, drips, and bristles of rough grain.

Take another long look at the inspirational designs and note how it is possible to decorate the yo-yo with all manner of moving and swirling patterns. Take a fine-point brush and the acrylic colors of your choice and lay on all the various lines, daubs, dots, and strokes that go to make up your chosen design (FIG. 1-2). Finally, when the acrylic paint is dry, lay on two more coats of varnish and, making sure that the cord is well clear of the sticky surfaces and the yo-yo is free from drips and runs, hang it up to dry.

HINTS

Make sure that you use a close-grained, knot-free, dry wood because if a dead knot should fall out or the wood should continue drying after the yo-yo has been turned, the yo-yo will be off-balance.

It makes good sense in terms of time, effort, and materials to make at least two yo-yos at the same time.

You could make the yo-yo in two halves and link them with a dowel, it's a thought!

With a small compact toy of this size, type, and character, it is most important that the wood is close-grained and the tools be sharp.

Make sure that the 1/8-inch-diameter core hole is centrally placed. It is important that the cord be a tight fixture; if it is allowed to slide around the core, the yo-yo won't work.

Making A Baby's
Ball-in-a-Cage
Rattle

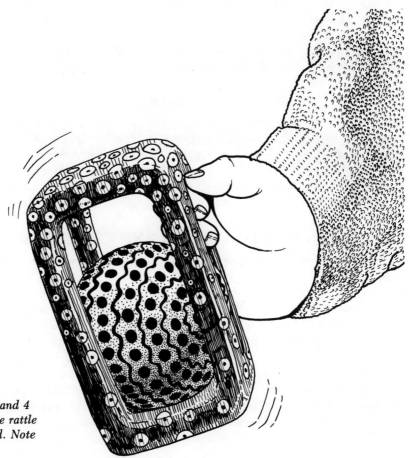

Fig. 2-1. At 2½ inches wide and 4 inches long, the ball-in-a-cage rattle is a good size for baby's hand. Note the smooth profile.

IN AMERICA AND IN SOME PARTS OF BRITAIN, THERE IS A FOLK TRADITION OF whittling and carving small trick items. Worked from single pieces of wood, such whittlings are not tricks in the sense that they can be played with or that they have a function, but rather puzzles because they look to be almost impossible to carve.

There are elaborate linked chains, curious fans and flowers, various hinged, jointed and linked love tokens, and of course the ball-in-a-cage type shakers and rattles. Carved from single hand-sized pieces of wood, all such enigmatic whittlings beg the same response and question: "That really is amazing! How did you do it?"

CONSIDERING THE PROJECT

Look at the working drawings and see how, in the context of this project, the ball-in-a-cage whittling is more than just a non-functional boast of skill, it also doubles as an exciting, decorative baby's rattle (FIGS. 2-1 and 2-3). With its smooth, rounded contours, and the fact that the captured ball is just waiting to be pushed, pulled, and rolled about, such a toy can't help but be a success. Look at the details, note how at a scale of four grid squares to 1 inch, the rattle is 2½ inches square and 4 inches long. Consider how the rattle ideally fulfills its function because it is the size of a hand, too large to be swallowed, completely nontoxic, and best of all, from the toy maker's point of view, it's a good, fun challenge.

TOOLS AND MATERIALS

You need ✦ A piece of lime, sycamore, or holly at 2½ × 2½ inches square and 4 inches long ✦ Workout paper ✦ Tracing paper ✦ A set square ✦ A pencil ✦ A ruler ✦ A pair of compasses ✦ A metal straight-edge ✦ A fine-point scalpel ✦ A selection of small penknives ✦ An oilstone ✦ A selection of colored felt-tip pens ✦ A small quantity of vegetable oil ✦ A fluff-free cloth

SETTING OUT THE DESIGN AND FIRST CUTS

Take the nicely squared and prepared block of wood and check it over for flaws. It needs to be smooth grained and completely free from knots and splits. With a set square, measure, metal rule, compass, and pencil, mark out the wood and set out all the margins and circles that go to make up the design (FIG. 2-4). Mark off all 2½- × 4-inch side faces with diagonals, and set out circles that are slightly less than 2½ inches in diameter. Draw on all side faces lines that are ½ inch in from the edges. Each of the four long faces should have a ½-inch-wide margins and a circle.

Now, bearing in mind that the whole point of the project is that the ball is larger than the width between the bars, take a penknife and set the drawn lines in with stop-cuts. Score lines around the margins and around the ball, and identify the areas of waste between the ball and the top and bottom of

Fig. 2-2. Painting grid. The scale is four grid squares to 1 inch. Use bright colors and bold forms.

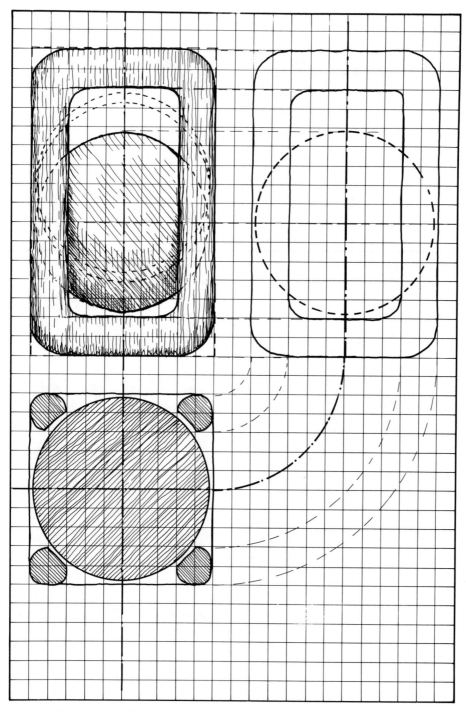

Fig. 2-3. Working drawing. The grid scale is four squares to 1 inch.

the cage. With deep paring cuts that are angled in toward the stop-cuts, gradually whittle and work deeper and deeper into the wood. And so you continue, running the point of the blade down either side of the bars and removing the waste until the square lump of wood within the bars is almost free to move.

Take the fine-point scalpel, and with the greatest care and caution, slice around the bars, from one face to another, to cut the ball-block free. Finally, work the bars along their length, and tidy up the top and bottom waste areas so that the ball-block is free to move.

SHAPING THE BALL AND CAGE INTERIOR

Now comes the tricky business of shaping the ball. Whittle away at the top and bottom corners of the block until the block begins to look more rounded. Being careful that the knife doesn't slip and split the grain, work with small, thumb-controlled slicing strokes until you are able to turn the ball around (FIG. 2-5). Continue working and nibbling away at the ball and the inside of the cage until you able to roll the ball freely in any direction. Be very careful that you don't reduce the size of the ball or increase the width between the bars. Bring the ball, the bars, and the inside ends of the cage to a good finish.

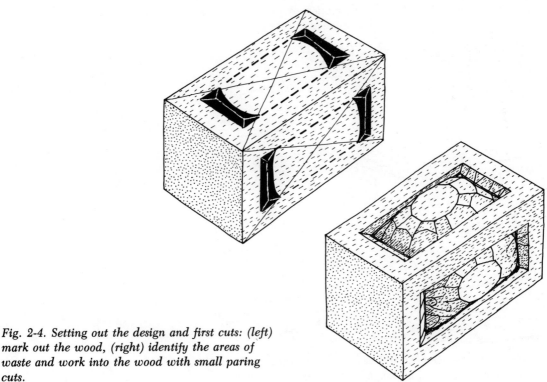

Fig. 2-4. Setting out the design and first cuts: (left) mark out the wood, (right) identify the areas of waste and work into the wood with small paring cuts.

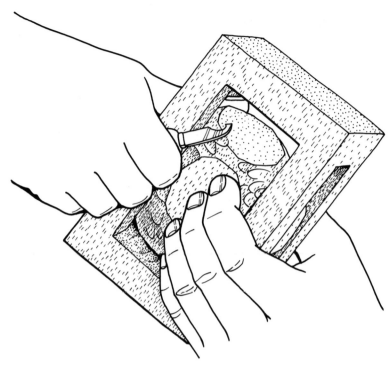

Fig. 2-5. Shaping the ball and cage interior. Work small, thumb-controlled slicing strokes until you are able to turn the ball around.

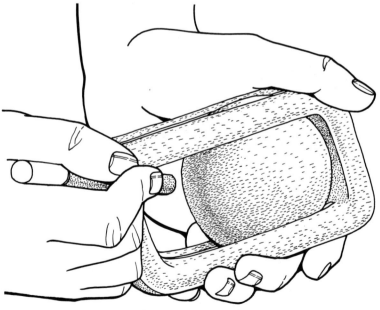

Fig. 2-6. Decorating and finishing. Rub the wood down until it is smooth and free from all roughnesses, splinters, and burrs.

DECORATING AND FINISHING

Working with or at an angle to the grain, cut away all sharp edges, angles, and corners until the whole block begins to look smooth and rounded. When you consider the ball and cage well whittled, take the graded sandpapers and rub down all surfaces. Now, working through the sandpapers from coarse to super-smooth, rub the wood down until the project is free from roughness, splinters, and burrs (FIG. 2-6).

Take the felt-tip pens and mark out and block in all the colors, forms, patterns, and motifs that go to make up your chosen design (FIG. 2-2). Finally, when the felt-tip colors are dry, rub the work down with a small amount of vegetable oil and burnish the wood to a smooth, shiny finish.

HINTS

It is most important that the rattle be the correct size and shape. If it's large and pointed, then it's dangerous; if it's small, then the child might decide to eat it. Bear such factors in mind if you do decide to modify the project.

When you are choosing the wood, go for a nontoxic, easy-to-carve, non-splinter type. Avoid dark woods that ooze color when wet.

Because children put things in their mouths, we have chosen to decorate the rattle using felt-tip pens and vegetable oil.

Making a
Diablo

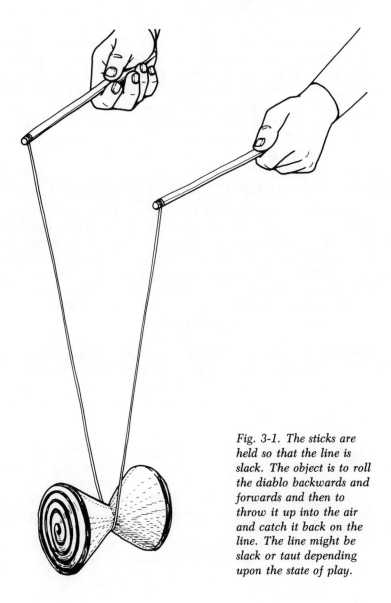

Fig. 3-1. The sticks are
held so that the line is
slack. The object is to roll
the diablo backwards and
forwards and then to
throw it up into the air
and catch it back on the
line. The line might be
slack or taut depending
upon the state of play.

FROM THE LATIN AND FRENCH WORDS *DIABLE* AND *DIABOLUS* MEANING magic, very difficult, or influenced by the devil, the game of diablo is, as the name suggests, very exciting but fiendishly difficult. You throw and catch a double-cone spinning top on a cord that is fastened to two hand-held sticks (FIG. 3-1). Adapted from the ancient game of *Devil on two sticks*, diablo is started by rolling the double-cone gently backwards and forwards on a slack string. Gradually the momentum of the spinning cone builds up so the string is pulled tighter and tighter until finally, when the cone looks to be spinning and whirling of its own accord, it is either tossed up into the air and caught, still spinning, on the player's own line, or the cone is thrown to another player. The object of the game is to keep the double-cone in motion as long as possible and to score the greatest number of successful throws.

Known in the fifteenth century as a *Flying Cone* or *Flying Devil*, and re-introduced into France and England in the eighteenth century, but this time known by its Chinese name of *Koengen*, diablo has from century to century been a popular game. Just as the craze for playing with yo-yos for no apparent reason, appears and disappears every 30 or 40 years, so the craze for playing with diablos swept across Europe in 1790, in 1820 and lastly, just before the First World war, in 1912. Could it be that your diablo is about to spark off the great diablo craze of the 1990s?

CONSIDERING THE PROJECT

When we first considered making a diablo, we had seen pictures of them in books, had seen them in museums, and had generally heard mention of them, but we had never actually touched one or seen one being used. We had certainly never played with one. The first thing I did was to rush out to my lathe and make a quick mock-up of a double-cone that in shape and size looked about right. When I tried to play with this prototype, I couldn't get it to work; it wouldn't stay on the string, it wouldn't roll or balance, in fact all in all it was worse than useless.

Thinking that perhaps the balance was wrong, I drilled out one side of the mock-up and used plastercine and lead pellets to make fine weight adjustments. Certainly my new improved model rolled along a taut cord, but no matter how hard I tried, I couldn't make it spin. I tried to *drive* the diablo by swiftly lowering and lifting alternate sticks. I tried swinging the sticks from side to side, but all to no avail. I just couldn't set it in positive motion.

Well, to cut a long and sorry tale short, I discovered, after a series of frustrating tryouts, that there are three main factors that make for a good diablo. First, it does need to be perfectly balanced, second, the central angle or drive groove must be sharp or at least tightly curved, and third, and perhaps most important of all, the cord needs to be made from a high-friction natural material like cotton, linen, or even leather.

Working through a whole range of cord and twine types—and at last getting so desperate that I finished up standing out in the rain trying to get the diablo to spin—I discovered that if the central groove is damp or at least unpolished and if the cord is rough or, better still, wet, then the friction between the wood and the cord allows the operator to drive the cone. Could it be that the diablo or the string needs to be chalked or powdered before use?

I also discovered that the cone isn't driven with a series of equal left and right pulls, this only results in the cone standing still, but rather it is *pulled* into motion with a slow passive left hand and a positive lift or jerk of the right hand.

The playing action is as follows: place the diablo across the cord and the cord on the ground; slowly raise both sticks in the left hand; take one stick in the right hand and raise it with a slightly flicking action, and the cone should roll with a counterclockwise spin toward the left hand. If you repeatedly lower and raise the left-hand stick, while at the same time lowering and jerking the right-hand stick, you will see that the cone gradually gets to be driven faster and faster in a counterclockwise direction. That is to say, the cone is *pulled* into motion or spun by the positive upward flick of the right hand.

Learning how to play with a diablo is made all the more difficult because the last craze swept England and America about 70 years ago and there are fewer and fewer people who even know what a diablo is, let alone played with one. This being so, start the project by having a good look at any diablos or pictures of diablos that you come across. Better still, if you do have aged friends or relatives, have a chat with them, it's just possible that they remember playing with this truly devilish toy and that they can pass on a few tips.

Finally, have a good look at the working drawings and the sections, and see how at a scale of four grid squares to 1 inch, our double-cone, round-ended diablo measures about 6 inches long by 3 inches wide at the shoulders and ½ inch wide at the neck. See how the form is turned between centers out of a single piece of wood. *Note*: You do of course need a pair of sticks to hang the cord, best if you use a couple of dowel lengths or bamboo canes, or turn a pair on the lathe to suit your needs.

TOOLS AND MATERIALS

You need ✦ A piece of close-grained knot-free easy to turn wood at about 4 inches × 4 inches square and 10 to 12 inches long; you might use holly, beech, box, kingwood, rosewood or another wood of your choice ✦ Work-out paper ✦ Tracing paper ✦ Template cardboard ✦ Pencil and ruler ✦ Scissors ✦ A pair of compasses ✦ A plane, rasp, or drawknife ✦ A center punch ✦ A hammer ✦ The use of a wood lathe ✦ A good selection of wood-turning tools ✦ A pair of calipers ✦ The use of a workbench and vise-clamp ✦ A straight saw ✦ A pack of graded sandpapers-glasspapers ✦ Masking tape ✦ A length of "painting" cord ✦ Varnish ✦ A selection of acrylic paints, colors to suit ◆ A selection of broad and fine-point, soft-haired, artist brushes ◆ A couple of 18-inch-long dowels, you might use bamboo canes ◆ About 72 inches of thick, strong cord—best to use linen or cotton

WORKING THE DESIGNS
AND
PREPARING THE WOOD

When you have seen various diablos in museums and when, if you are lucky, you have seen a diablo being used, then have a good long look at our working drawings and details. See that at a scale of four grid squares to 1 inch, the double-cone diablo is about 5½ inches long, 3 inches wide at the shoulders, and ½ inch wide at the neck (FIGS. 3-2 and 3-3). It's worth noting at this stage that we have seen museum diablos of just about every conceivable shape and size, so if you have a fancy to modify our design and have more decorations, a chunkier form, a sharper angle at the neck, or whatever, no matter, the diablo will work as long as you stay within the overall form, shape, material, and angle limits.

Bearing all these pointers in mind, draw up your designs to size. Take a tracing and press transfer the traced lines through to the template card (FIG. 3-4).

When you have cut out the three forms that go to make up the total template profile, try a trial draw-around on some scrap paper and see how a template needs to be used in conjunction with a pair of calipers.

The templates made, draw diagonals across the ends of your chosen length of squared-up wood and then, with punch and hammer, establish the center points, or the points of spin.

Now, with pencil ruler and a pair of compasses, mark off the ends of the wood with 3-inch-diameter circles, draw tangents across the diagonals and run lines from the points of the resultant octagons down the length of the wood.

Finally, with a plane, rasp or knife, swiftly remove most of the corner waste but don't try to cut right back to the 3-inch-diameter circle, just settle for cutting off the sharp corners.

TURNING THE CYLINDER

Having set the wood between lathe centers, give it a sharp tap with the mallet to drive it onto the fork center at the left end of the lathe. When the drive end of the wood is in place, wind up the tailstock until it is forced well into the wood, then ease off slightly and drip a little oil into the right-hand, dead center hole. This done, bring the T-rest up, set it as close as possible to the work and fix it at about lathe center height.

Now pin up your designs and arrange all your tools so they are available but well clear of the lathe. Roll up your sleeves, generally make sure that your tie, hair, ribbon, necklace, or whatever is well out of harm's way. Make a last check to verify that the lathe is in good order, then turn the switch

Fig. 3-2. *Painting grid. Best to set the cone ends out with vigorous "moving and turning" motifs, patterns, and designs.*

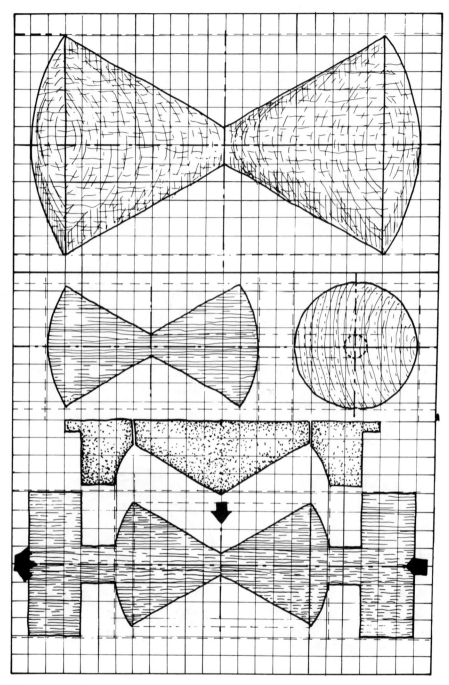

Fig. 3-3. Working drawing. The scale is four grid squares to 1 inch (top). Note
how the template needs to be cut down into three pieces. It is most important
that the form be well balanced.

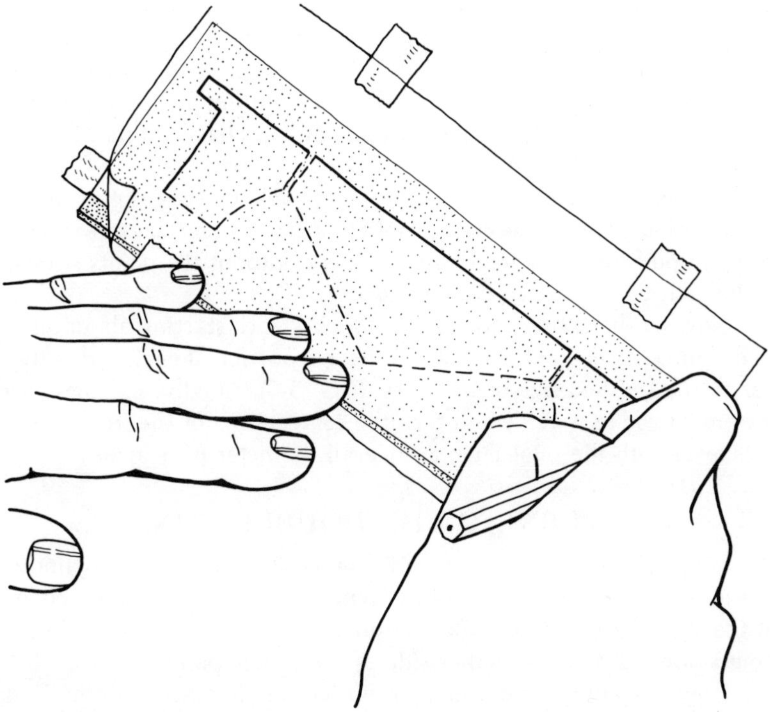

Fig. 3-4. Working the designs and preparing the wood. Press transfer the traced lines through to the template card. Secure both the card and the tracing with tabs of masking tape.

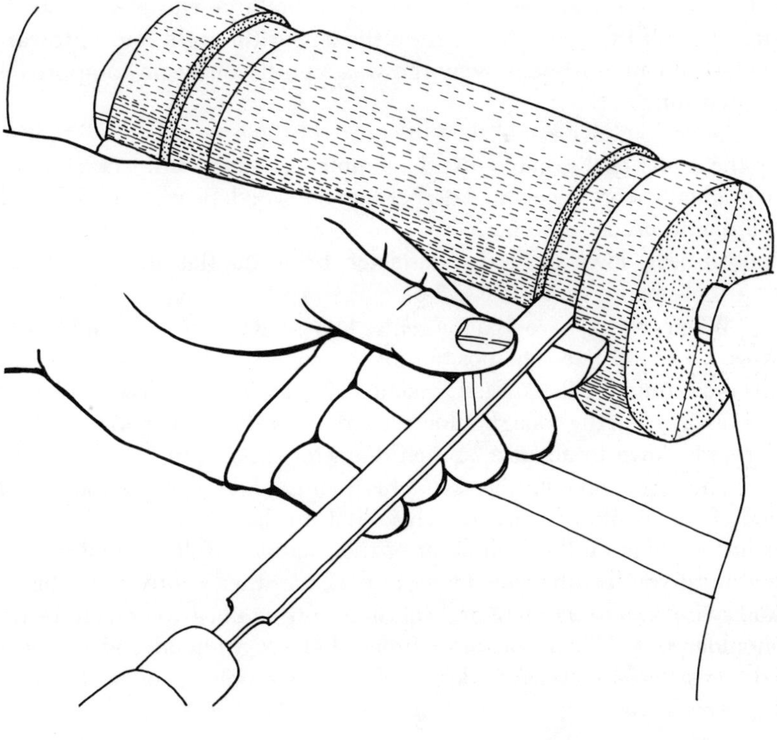

Fig. 3-5. Turning the cylinder. Cut back a portion at each end. Aim for a finished diameter size of 3 inches.

on. *Note*: If you feel at all worried about getting wood dust in your eyes or hair, consider wearing a visor or a pair of goggles and a hat.

Take up the round nosed chisel, hold it against the rest so the handle is ever-so-slightly tilted upward and start stripping away the rough. Work backward and forward along the wood until you have cut past the flats and until you have achieved an overall round section.

As soon as all unevenness has been cut back, set the calipers to $3\frac{1}{4}$ inches and gradually continue cutting until this diameter has been reached. When you can push the calipers across the work without the points sticking, the cylinder is $3\frac{1}{4}$ inches in diameter.

Now set the calipers to exactly 3 inches and, starting about an inch or so in from each end of the wood, cut back a portion at each end of the cylinder to the finished size of 3 inches (FIG. 3-5). Finally, use these areas of lowered wood as a guide and turn the central area of the stock down until it is level with the pilot cuts, an overall diameter of 3 inches.

TURNING THE DOUBLE CONE

When you have turned off a nicely worked 3-inch-diameter cylinder, take a pencil and ruler and mark off the center point, the maximum cone width at the shoulders, and the ends. The maximum cone width should occur at points about $2\frac{1}{4}$ inches either side of the center point.

Now, remember that you must not cut against the grain and take the tool of your choice and start to turn out the point-to-point double-cone form (FIG. 3-6). Work and slide the tool from the large end of the cone to the small end of the cone (that is from the left or the right and in toward the center) to cautiously cut away the waste until you begin to approach the desired form.

Once you have established the angle of the broad flat "V" that makes up the center of the diablo, use the templates and the calipers set at $\frac{1}{2}$ inch to gradually work deeper and deeper into the wood. Bear in mind that ideally the diablo needs to be perfectly symmetrical. When you have turned the central neck down to $\frac{1}{2}$-inch-diameter, bring the flat angled central area to a tool-smooth finish (FIG. 3-6).

When you have worked the center to a good template fit and finish, and when you have fixed the position of the cone shoulders and ends, start to cut the terminal curves. First, take a $\frac{1}{2}$-inch wide flat chisel and, working well away from the cone shoulders, clear away the waste and turn the cylinder ends down to about a $\frac{1}{2}$-inch diameter (FIG. 3-6).

This done, take up the skew chisel and, while working the right-hand end of the diablo first, lay the chisel flat on the tool rest so that the bevel is just rubbing on the high point of the shoulder. Roll the tool toward the end until you feel the edge begin to bite, and then gently raise the handle and swing it in to the right and continue cutting until you reach the desired shoulder line. When you have finished the right-hand end of the cone, complete the left-hand shoulders in like manner, only of course this time turn the skew chisel over and work in the opposite direction.

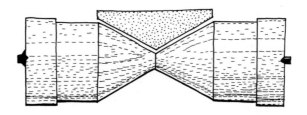

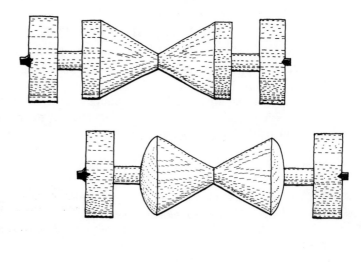

Fig. 3-6. Turning the doublecone: (top) use a template to achieve an accurate center point; (middle) clean away the side/end waste; (bottom) cut and curve the shoulder profile.

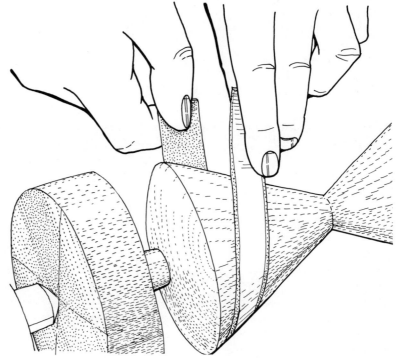

Fig. 3-7. Turning the double cone. Take the graded sandpapers and rub the spinning wood down to a good finish.

When you consider the form well turned and when you have checked and double-checked all the sizes, angles, and curves with the templates and the calipers, take the graded sandpapers and glasspapers and rub the spinning wood down to a good finish (FIG. 3-7). Now take the parting tool and cut-in each end; that is, cut in as far as you can without actual separation. Finally, remove the wood from the lathe and complete the separation by securing the straight saw upside down in the vise and by running the work back and forth across the teeth.

FINISHING AND PAINTING

Set the diablo across a taut cord and see how it is for balance. If one end or other is slightly heavy, take a piece of coarse grade sandpaper and, being careful not to spoil the shape of the curve, try to reduce the wood at that point. And so you continue, testing and sanding until you have achieved, as near as possible, perfect balance. This done, clear away the clutter, make sure that the diablo is free from dust and set out your varnish, paints, and brushes.

Wrap a piece of ½-inch-wide masking tape around the central V neck of the diablo and string it up for painting (FIG. 3-8). Lay on thin coat of varnish, then use a fine-point brush and acrylic colors to pick out the various swirls and patterns that go to make up the design, and lay on another coat of varnish. Don't forget to let the varnish and paint dry out between coats.

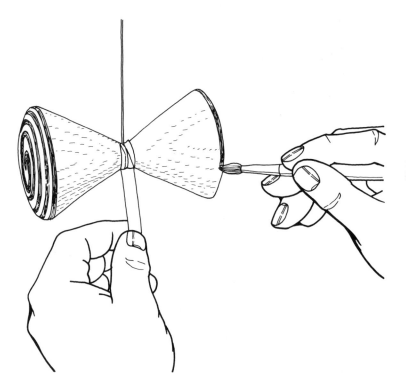

Fig. 3-8. Finishing and painting. Wrap a piece of ½-inch-wide masking tape around the central V neck and hang the diablo on a cord. Steady the work by holding the tape.

Finally, when the varnish is dry, peel off the masking tape to reveal the unvarnished high-friction area and knot the length of special cord to the two stick ends, and you are ready for the face off!

HINTS

Bear in mind that size, weight, balance, and form are critical, you might experiment by making several prototypes with an inexpensive wood.

When you have made the diablo and you are ready for your first tryout, make sure that you are well clear of windows and traffic. Best to play in the garden or park.

You might take the project a little further and make two sticks on the lathe.

Making an
Indoors
Skittle Game

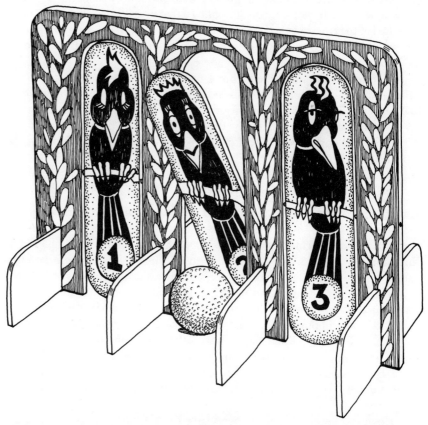

Fig. 4-1. The object of the game is to roll the ball through the trap to knock the bird over on his pivot and to reveal the number/bird on the other side, to the next player's advantage or disadvantage.

CHILDREN FIND A GREAT DEAL OF PLEASURE IN PLAYING WITH *KNOCK-OVER* skittle indoor toys, which are toys that involve setting up a number of blocks, soldiers, skittles, cards, or whatever, and then knocking them down with a ball, a popgun, or a quoit (a ring). I remember, as a child of about eight years of age, I had two such toys. One was an old Victorian game of table skittles. It had turned and beaded figures, and a swivel-top pole with a ball hanging on a string. All this was arranged on a beautiful polished, gold-numbered, darkwood board. Of course it was good fun to throw the ball so that it scythed the figures down, but as I remember, the best bit was not so much knocking the men down, but rather setting them back up again. Underneath the board, in a secret lidded cavity, there was a complex web of cords that ran from the individual skittles, through holes in the board to a ratcheted handle. As the massive handle was turned, all the little figures slowly shuddered, stood up, and wobbled to attention!

Perhaps the better knock-over toy was a strange game called something like *Three Black Crows.* Made of wood and tin sheet, there was a cork-firing popgun and an arched shooting gallery with three crow-decorated targets set on a pivotal wire. At a range of about 10 feet or so, when the corks found their target the tin crows would flip backwards, to reveal—depending upon the striking force of the cork—the same crow, or one that was painted on the other side of the sheet.

The crows were numbered from 1 to 6 and the object was not only to achieve the highest score, but also to tip the crows over on their pivots so that higher or lower numbers on the other side were revealed to the advantage or disadvantage of the next player. With the crows twirling round like windmills and corks zooming all over the room, this was not a toy for the faint hearted!

CONSIDERING THE PROJECTS

Have a look at the project picture and the various working drawings and see how the 12- × -18-inch main board and the four slotted 6- × -3-inch supports can all be cut from a single 18- × -18-inch-square sheet of ⅜-inch-thick multi-ply (FIGS. 4-1 and 4-3). With all the curves being worked to a radius of 1½ inches, and with the arched form standing on easy-to-fit feet, this toy has the added bonus that it can be easily set up, and just as easily packed flat and popped back into the cupboard. The perfect toy for small compact modern homes and "What-a-horrible-mess-your-room's-in" children.

We have also modified the design so that the game now relates to the use of soft tennis balls rather than guns. Of course if you don't like the imagery, or you have a passion for air guns, marbles, or whatever, then there's no reason why you can't change the targets and the missiles to suit your own interests.

However, before you start spend time finding out as much as you can about traditional indoor skittle toys. Visit toy museums, talk to old people, and look through prewar toy books and catalogues. Lastly, draw up plans and finalize all the measurements and details that go to make up the design.

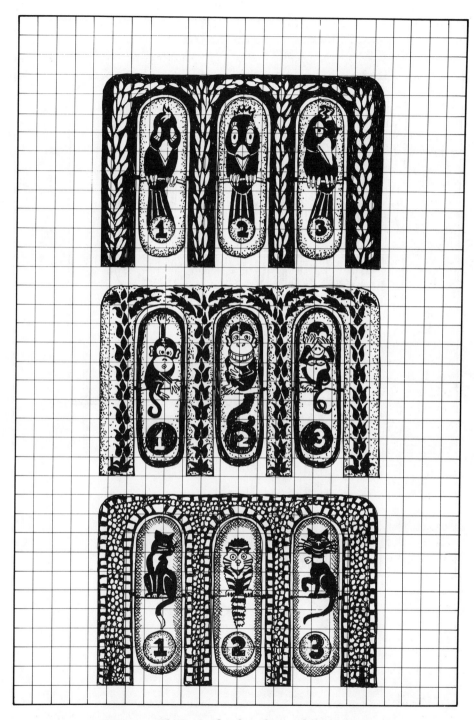

Fig. 4-2. Painting grid. Go for bright colors and bold and direct forms.

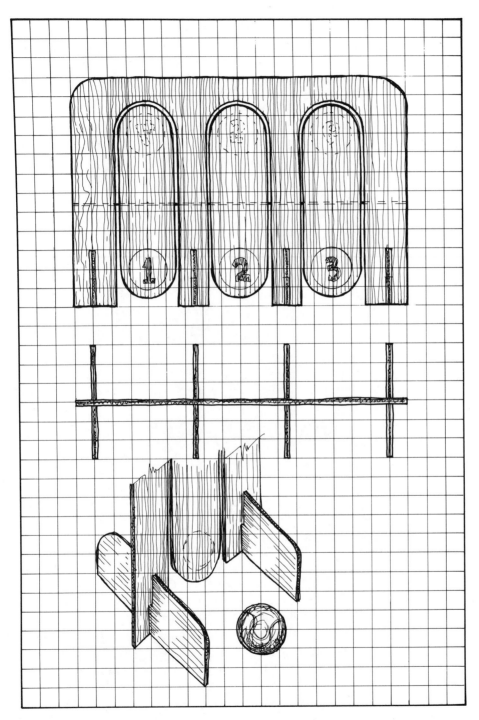

Fig. 4-3. Working drawing. At a scale of one grid square to 1 inch the main board is 12 inches high and 18 inches wide (top). Note the simple slot fixings.

TOOLS AND MATERIALS

You need ✦ An 18-×-18-inch sheet of best quality multi-ply at ⅜-inch thickness ✦ Workout paper ✦ Tracing paper ✦ A pencil and ruler ✦ A workbench with a vise ✦ A set square ✦ A pair of compasses ✦ A small straight saw ✦ A coping saw ✦ A rasp-type shaping tool ✦ A pack of graded sandpapers ✦ A hand drill with a ⅛-inch-diameter drill bit ✦ A pair of pliers ✦ An 18-inch length of ⅛-inch-thick wire ✦ A small amount of resin glue ✦ A good selection of acrylic paints, colors to suit ✦ A tin of clear varnish ✦ Brushes and odds and ends like cloths, paint tubs, and newspapers

SETTING OUT THE DESIGN AND FRETTING THE WOOD

When you have weighed up all the pros and cons of the project, and when you have a good clear picture in your mind's eye of how you want your skittle game to be, draw the various designs out to size and finalize all the measurements and profiles (FIG. 4-4). Carefully trace off the lines of the design then, with pencil, ruler, compass, and set square, transfer the lines through to the working face of the plywood. Check measurements, make sure lines are square, and generally see to it that the forms are well set out and accurate. When you have checked and double-checked that all is correct, set to work with the straight saw and the coping saw, and fret out the eight forms that go to make up the design. It's all easy and straightforward; just make sure that you hold the saw so that the blade cuts the wood at right angles to the working face. Work at a steady, even pace, all the time trying to keep the saw blade a little to the waste side of the drawn lines.

When you cut out the three arches, take it that the line of next cut is on the inside-arch side of the drawn line. If you work the two outside arches first and finish up with the one in the center, then you won't have problems trying to maneuver the saw frame (FIG. 4-5).

Finally, when you have fretted out the eight forms—the arched board, the three targets, and the four feet—and when you have cut all eight 1½-inch-long ¼-inch-wide fitting slots, take the graded sandpapers and rub all the cut edges down to a good smooth finish.

FITTING THE PIVOT WIRE

With the target cut-outs set in their arches and with the whole project arranged flat and faceup on the workbench, mark in a point 6⅜ inches up on each side of the arched frame. Link the two points with a straightedge and draw in a line that runs across the four arch legs and the three targets; make sure that this pivot wire line is correctly and clearly established. Next comes the difficult task of running a drill hole through the middle of the ⅜-inch plywood thickness. Securely set the target cut-outs a piece at a time

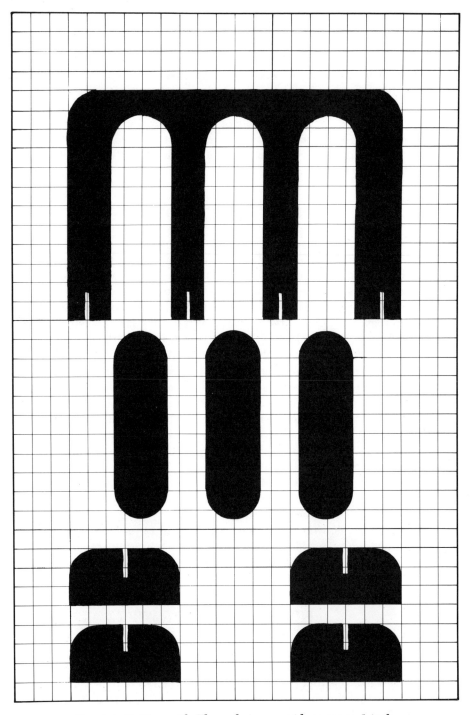

Fig. 4-4. Cutting grid. The scale is one grid square to 1 inch.

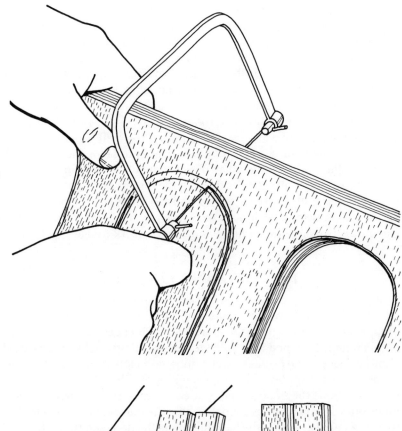

Fig. 4-5. Setting out the designs and fretting the wood. Cut the two outside arches first. Run the saw down on the "inside arch" side of the drawn line.

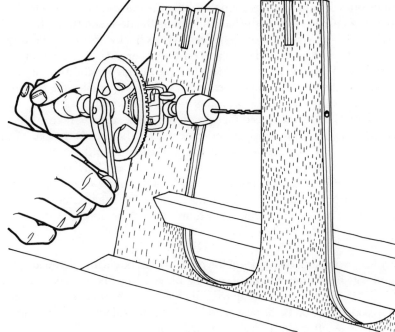

Fig. 4-6. Fitting the pivot wire. Bend the "legs" out of the way so that you can drill the pivot holes.

in the jaws of a vise. Make sure that the drill bit is perfectly aligned with the drawn line and with the face of the plywood, then bore the holes out. The drill bit might be too short to run through the full width of the wood. If this is the case, turn the cut-out around in the vise and drill from the other edge. When it is time to drill the holes through the legs of the arches, the problems get a little more tricky because not only do you have to approach each arch leg from opposite edges, but you also have to bend other arch legs out of the way so that you have room to work (FIG. 4-6). Take it slowly and carefully, all the while making sure that the drill is perfectly aligned. If you have any doubts, ask a couple of friends to help: one friend to keep an eye on the drill, and the other friend to hold the wood out of the way. Aim for easy, loose-fitting holes through the targets and tight holes through the arch legs. With the holes drilled and the three targets in position, run the ⅛-inch-diameter wire through the whole project. Finally, dab a little resin glue in the two end-of-wire holes and put the work to one side to dry out.

PAINTING AND FINISHING

When all three targets have been threaded on the pivotal wire and when the resin glue is dry, give the whole project a rub down with a fine-grade sandpaper. Make sure that there are no rough edges, wipe the wood over with a damp cloth, and then move to the area that you have organized for painting. Set out the brushes, paints, tubs, and cloths, and then have another look at our inspirational designs and ideas (FIG. 4-2).

Note how the motifs and patterns are painted directly onto an undecorated plain wood ground. See how the numbers and the motifs need to be organized so that as the ball rolls along the floor and through the target arch—and as the bottom of the target swivels backwards and the front tips forwards—the motifs and numbers on the other side of the target appear correctly. When you have considered all the design possibilities, finalize the details on the workout paper, trace off, and then pencil-press transfer the traced lines through to the working face of the wood (FIG. 4-7).

With the project placed face-up on the work surface, take a fine-point brush and your chosen colors and pick out all the details that go to make up your design. Bear in mind that the pattern and motif details need to be clearly visible even at a distance of about 10 to 12 feet. Stay away from fussy, subtle colors and details, but rather go for bold black-edged forms, bright striking primary colors, and crisp naive imagery. Finally, lay on a couple of coats of hard-gloss yacht varnish and the job is done.

HINTS

If you care to paint both sides of the main arched board and if you are playing with soft balls, then the game can be played from both sides.

If you think it too difficult to drill holes right through a piece of on-edge plywood, then modify the design and have the pivotal wire or wires supported either by small metal U fixings or with blocks.

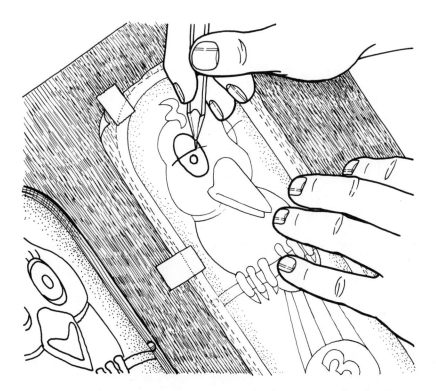

Fig. 4-7. Painting and finishing. Pencil-press transfer the traced lines through to the working face of the wood.

We have numbered the targets, from left to right, 1, 2, 3 on one side and 4, 5, 6 on the other. If you change the last sequence to 6, 5, 4, so that the highest and lowest numbers occur on the same target, then a player might go for the highest number but get the lowest. Such an arrangement makes for a more exciting game. If the targets are numbered this way, the total score for each target adds up to 7. Maybe the rules of the game could be shaped to take this into account.

Making a
Skipping Rope

Fig. 5-1. Girl with a skipping
rope inspired by an illustration
from Kate Greenaway's nineteenth century book "Birthday
Book For Children."

FROM THE OLD NORSE WORDS *SKOPA* AND *SKUPPA*, MEANING "TO TAKE A run" and "to jump from one foot to the other" and "to move about with a series of light bounds, hops, and capers," we have the beautiful word *skip*. The word has now come to describe a light-hearted gamboling activity. In this context, a skipping rope is a cord having handles, as used in the children's game of skipping. Of course a skipping rope isn't necessarily exciting in itself because it doesn't move, whistle, bounce, or buzz. Rather it is, just like a hoop or a spinning top, a medium through which more complex dancing, twirling, and singing games can be played (FIG. 5-1).

The game of rope skipping is one of those mysterious, almost magical, activities that is as old as time itself. If we could go back to ancient Rome, or visit a South Sea island, we would almost certainly find one or more children skipping. When I was a child of say about five or six, I well remember that skipping was one of those school playground games that could be played by boys and girls alike. A couple of hefty lads would hold and swing the rope while the girls would take turns ducking, jumping, and skipping.

To help the game along there were rhythmic, repetitive chants. One such song went something like:

"Salt, mustard, vinegar, pepper—salt, mustard, vinegar, pepper—salt . . ." and so on adinfinitum. And then again, there are much older and more meaningful songs like:

"Sally, Sally Waters,
Sprinkle in the pan,
Rise Sally, rise Sally,
Choose a young man.
Bow to the east,
Bow to the west,
Bow to the young man
That you love best."

While the rope was being swung in time to the chant, the girl in the middle, still skipping, had to invite another girl or a boy in to join her. The whole object of the game was to try and finish up with as many children as possible all skipping and singing under the swinging rope.

Of course if one or other of the children tripped over the rope, then all hell was let loose and the game had to be started over. Skipping is good fun and a good skipping rope, one with brightly painted handles, was and perhaps still is a prestigious status toy. This being so, why don't you make the favorite child in your life such a rope?

CONSIDERING THE PROJECT

At first sight you might think that making a couple of turned skipping-rope handles is so easy and inconsequential that really it isn't worth the bother. That's hardly the case. Have a look at the inspirational designs and the work-

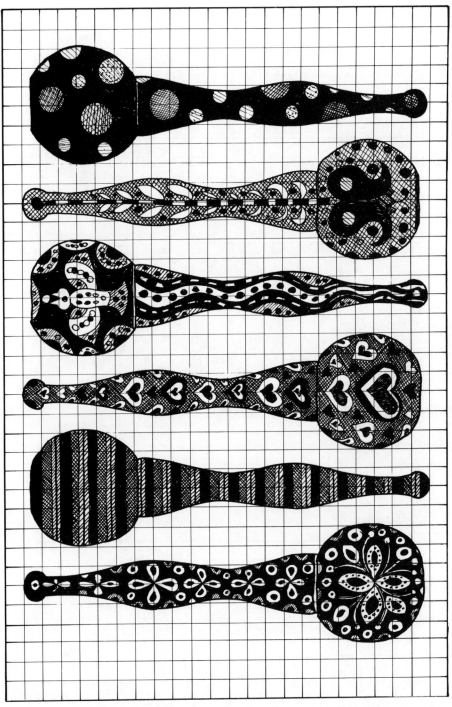

Fig. 5-2. Painting grid. The grid scale is approximately three squares to 1 inch. Use strong forms and juicy colors.

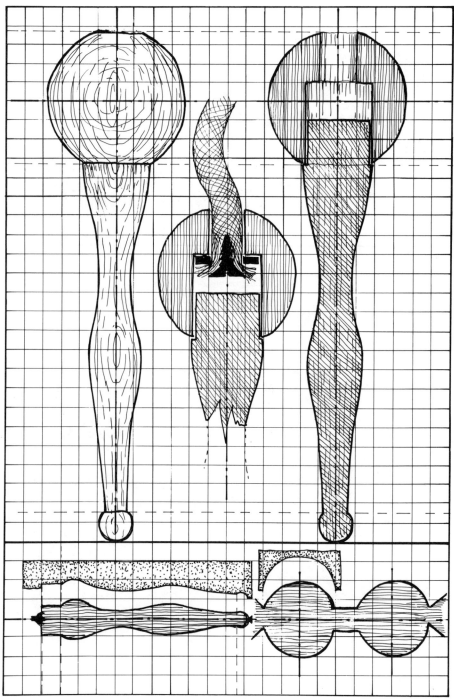

Fig. 5-3. Working drawing. At a grid scale of four squares to 1 inch, the handle is about 6½ inches long. Note the screw-and-washer fixing of the rope, and the spigot-to-ball fit of the handle.

ing drawings and see how there is more to this project than first meets the eye (FIGS. 5-1 and 5-2).

For example, each handle is made up of two turnings, a ball and a spigoted bobbin. And the cord isn't just glued or knotted; it's cunningly fixed in the ball recess with a washer and screw (FIG. 5-3).

And as for the painted designs, who could resist a skipping rope with handles all painted with love hearts and candy stripes, or with Pennsylvania Dutch tulips and birds (FIG. 5-2)?

If you are looking to make a good and solid traditional toy, then this project is well worth consideration. All this is not to say that the techniques are complex, only that turning identical forms is a bit tricky and turning one shape to fit within another does require extra care and attention.

However, have a look at the working drawings and see how—at a scale of four grid squares to 1 inch—the handles measure about 5 inches from ball to bobbin end and about 2 inches across the ball. Of course if you want to make handles that are bigger, or ones that are smaller, or whatever, then all you need do is to scale the designs up or down accordingly.

See if you can pick up extra hints, ideas and pointers by visiting museums and toy shops. Don't be content to search out skipping rope handles, but rather have a look at a whole range of objects that have, perhaps only in part, been turned. There are push carts with plump handles, long and slender gouge handles, dolls with turned legs, curvy bobbin dolls, skittle dolls, curved and beaded chair legs, and so on. There are any number of exciting inspirational possibilities.

Finally, once you have spent time searching out and analyzing the various forms, all the dips, curves, beads, tapers and swellings, and once you have considered extending and modifying the project, then you can draw the designs up to size. Keep in mind when designing, that the handles must be comfortable to hold.

TOOLS AND MATERIALS

You need ✦ Three pieces of easy-to-turn wood, one piece at 2 inches square and about 9 to 10 inches long for the two balls, and another two pieces at about 1¼ inches square and 7 inches long for the two bobbins. You also need ✦ Workout paper ✦ Pencils ✦ A pair of compasses ✦ A ruler ✦ Thin plywood ✦ A workbench and vise ✦ A coping saw ✦ A center punch ✦ A surform rasp ✦ The use of a wood turning lathe ✦ A good selection of wood-turning tools ✦ A pair of calipers ✦ A brace drill ✦ Two drill bits, a 1-inch-diameter Forstner or auger, and an ordinary bit at ½ inch ✦ A pack of graded sandpapers ✦ Two 1-inch-diameter washers ✦ A couple of short, fat wood screws, best if they are made of brass ✦ A screw driver ✦ A length of ½-inch-thick, cotton covered, braided rope, length to suit ✦ PVA wood glue ✦ Clear sticky tape ✦ Masking tape ✦ Primer and undercoat ✦ Gloss enamel paints, colors to suit ✦ A selection of broad- and fine-point, soft-haired artist brushes

TURNING THE BALLS

When you have drawn up and established your designs, take tracings and press-transfer the traced lines through to the thin template plywood. Set the plywood securely in the jaws of the vise and—bearing in mind that the blade needs to be held at right angles to the working face of the wood and that you need to cut on the waste side of the drawn lines—take the coping saw and carefully fret out the two template forms. Use the sandpaper to bring the various curves of the templates to a perfect fit and finish.

Take your chosen piece of 2-inch-square, 10-inch-long wood, draw out diagonals on the square-cut ends, use the punch to establish the center-points, then secure it between lathe centers. Use the surform rasp to swiftly cut away the bulk of the waste, then set out the tools, check that the lathe is in good order, and switch on.

Swiftly turn the wood down to a cylinder that is a fraction under 2 inches in diameter. With the measure, calipers, and parting tool, mark the wood off at 2-inch intervals. Take a small gouge, hold it on its back at right angles to the wood being worked, and turn away the waste (FIG. 5-4).

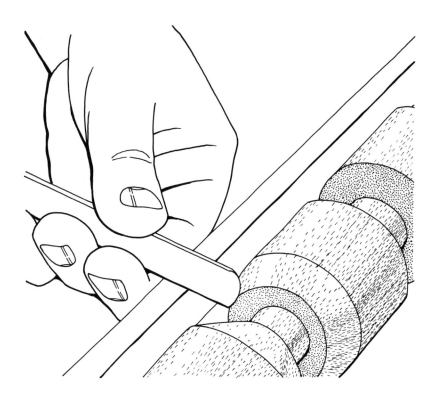

Fig. 5-4. Turning the balls. Take the small gouge, hold it on its back and at right angles to the work, and turn away the waste.

Work along the wood from left to right. Taper in for 2 inches. Leave 2 inches for the first ball. Clear away 2 inches of central waste. Leave 2 inches for the second ball, and lastly taper in for 2 inches. Take the skew chisel, and working the balls from center-to-side, start to turn off the curves. Be sure to stop the lathe before you check for size and fit, then continue turning until you have achieved the two identical spherical forms. Finally, use the sandpaper to bring the wood to a good finish and carefully part off.

DRILLING OUT THE ROPE AND SPIGOT HOLES

Have a good look at the working drawing sections and note how each ball needs to be drilled twice, once for the ½-inch rope and once for the 1-inch-diameter handle spigot, then set your turnings a piece at a time and cut-side up in the jaws of a cloth-muffled vise. With the wood secure, take the 1-inch-diameter Forstner bit and bore out a 1-inch-deep hole (FIG. 5-5). Center the ½-inch-diameter drill bit in the base of the 1-inch-diameter sinking and run a hole straight through the ball. Work with caution and be careful that the drill doesn't burst through and split the wood.

TURNING THE BOBBIN HANDLES

Study the working drawings and see how the bobbin handles need to be turned and worked so that the broad end, that is the end with the stepped spigot, is a good tight fit in the 1-inch-wide ball hole.

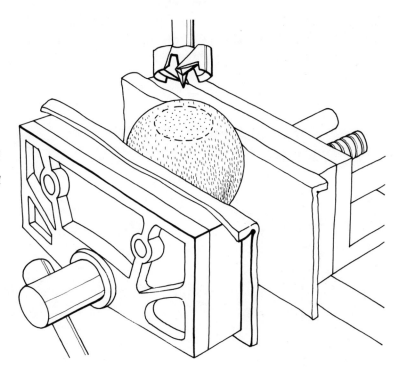

Fig. 5-5. Drilling out the rope and spigot holes. Secure the wood in the jaws of a muffled vise and bore a 1-inch-diameter hole with a Forstner bit.

Bear in mind that you have to make two identical bobbins. Take the 7-inch-long piece of wood and give it a quick check over just to make sure that it is free from splits and loose knots. Assume that the ends are square and mark diagonals at each end and inscribe 1¼-inch-diameter circles. Punch in the center-points, rasp off the waste, and set the wood securely between lathe centers. Position the tool rest so that it is as close as possible to the work and slightly below centerline and switch on.

Use the round-nosed chisel to clear away the rough, and work the wood backwards and forwards until you have achieved an overall smooth 1¼-inch-diameter cylinder. Now, with pencil, ruler, calipers, template, and a parting tool, mark out the position of the various hollows and steps that go to make up the form (FIG. 5-6). Make a mark at the spigot shoulder, at the center of the concave curves, and at the end knob (or finial).

Make a pilot cut at the center of each hollow to register the depth, then take a round-nosed chisel—a chisel that is smaller in width than the hollow—and work it slowly from side to side. Aim to gradually increase the width and depth of the hollow. And so you continue until all the dips and curves are well turned.

Note that the spigot needs to be about ½-inch long and a tight fit in the 1-inch-diameter ball hole, then take a square chisel and turn the wide end of the bobbin to size. Finally, sand the spinning wood down to a smooth finish, take the wood from the lathe, and use the saw to part off.

FITTING, FINISHING, AND PAINTING

Once you have achieved two push-fit balls-and-bobbin handles, then comes the slightly tricky business of fitting the rope. Cut the rope to length—this might be anything from six to eight feet, depending upon the age and height

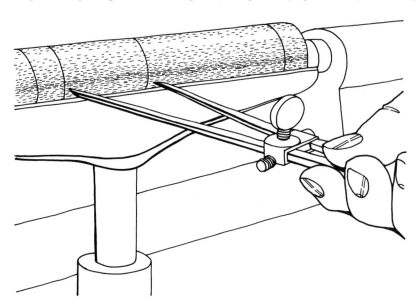

Fig. 5-6. Turning the bobbin handle. Turn down to a cylinder and mark out the position of all the hollows and steps.

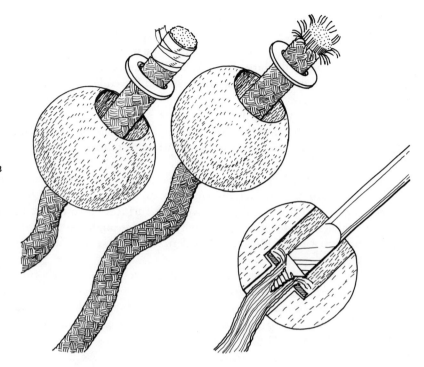

Fig. 5-7. Fitting, finishing, and painting. Thread the rope through the hole, push the washer over the end of the rope, remove the tape, and thread the screw hard up against the washer.

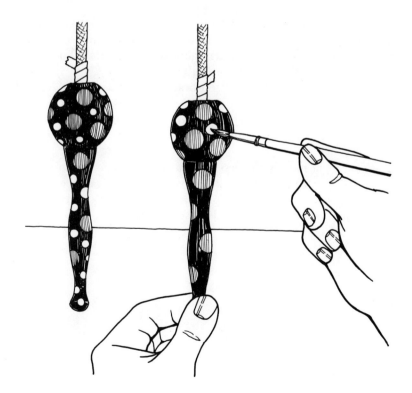

Fig. 5-8. Fitting, finishing, and painting. Protect the rope with a wrap of masking tape and use a fine-point brush to paint on all the details that go to make your chosen design.

of the person for whom the rope is intended—and bind each end with a few turns of clear sticky tape. One end at a time, thread the rope through the ½-inch-diameter ball hole—that is push the rope up through the ball so that the end comes out of the large hole. Take the washer and push it over the end of the rope. Remove the sticky tape, spread the end of the rope to find its center, then thread the short stubby wood screw tight into the rope and hard up against the washer (FIG. 5-7).

Pull the rope back into the ball and when the washer is a tight firm fit at the bottom of the ball hole, dribble a little glue onto the bobbin spigot and push it home.

When the glue is dry, take the skipping rope to the painting area, mask off the rope to protect it from paint smudges, and hang it up so the handles are well apart and just clear of the working surface. Have a look at the inspirational designs, see how variously the handles might be painted with all manner of exciting traditional and modern designs, then set out your colors and brushes.

Swiftly lay on and let dry a primer and undercoat, then take a full soft-haired brush and your chosen ground color and lay on a generous gloss coat. Finally, when the ground color is dry, take the fine-point brush and the contrasting colors and paint on all the dots, dashes, and daubs that go to make up the design (FIG. 5-8).

HINTS

If you have plenty of wood and a long-bed lathe, the two balls and the two handles might all be turned out of a piece of one length of wood.

If you have a screw-box, you might make it so that the bobbin is a screw fit in the ball, rather than have it glued.

The rope needs to be of the soft braided cotton-type used on yachts and dinghies.

The rope ends could be knot-fixed rather than screwed.

If you have plenty of paint you might consider dip-painting, rather than brushing.

You might modify the design to incorporate one or more bells. These might be set within the balls or screwed to the ends of the handles.

Many adults now skip for pleasure and in an effort to keep fit—with this in mind, perhaps you could make a skipping rope for the *big* boy or girl in your life.

Making a Pull-Along
Moving Toy

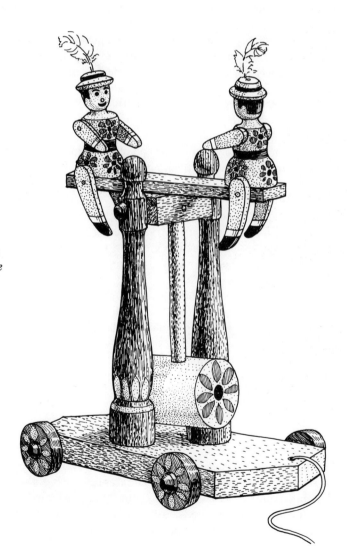

Fig. 6-1. As the toy is pulled along, so the pendulum is set in motion with the result that the two figures bob up and down on their see-saw.

WHEELED PULL-ALONG TOYS DATE BACK TO THE INVENTION OF THE WHEEL itself, in fact it has even been suggested that full-size vehicles were inspired by such toys, with small carts and trucks being, as it were, prototypes for the real thing. There were pull-along animals in ancient Egypt; the Romans and Greeks made little wooden chariots; the Chinese made wheeled pull-along farmyard animals, and so I could continue. From country to country and age to age, craftsmen—sometimes professional toymakers, but more often than not, simply interested parties like parents and grandparents—have found expression in making simple, wooden, pull-along, moving toys.

Of course, all ethnic folk art toys have some feature or other that sets them apart and makes them special. It might be the way they are carved, the delicate structure, the unusual imagery, the colors, the patterns, or whatever, but to my way of thinking, the turned, carved, and painted, pull-along wheeled moving toys—as were made by the peasants in eighteenth and nineteenth century Germany—are something extra special.

As to where the rural toymakers of the German districts of Thuringia, Nuremberg, Oberammergau, and Berchtesgaden drew the inspiration for their wonderful ingenious toys, perhaps the isolated, mountainous environment with its rushing rivers and deep dark forests was in itself inspiration! Who can say?

It's enough to know that by the end of the eighteenth century, *Nuremberg* and *Berchtesgaden* wares, meaning wooden toys in general and pull-along automata in particular, were being exported all over the world.

This unique folk art, country-rustic, wooden-toymaking tradition is characterized by carved, turned, and painted, farm carts, animals, women with babies in cradles, Noah's Arks, rocking horses, carriages, musicians, soldiers, and acrobats. They are mounted on wheels and worked in a way that has been described variously as naive, unsophisticated, architypal, and primitive.

What child or woodworking parent could not find pleasure in a pull-along toy that features, for example, such moving and whirling delights as figures that dance or bob up and down, horses that jog, and acrobats that tumble!

If you are looking to make a traditional all-wood, mechanical, trundle, pull-along toy—one that involves such woodworking pleasures as woodturning, carving, peg-jointing, and painting—then this is the project for you! (FIG. 6-1)

CONSIDERING THE PROJECT

Have a good long look at the illustrations and working drawings and sections and see how, at a grid scale of three squares to 2 inches, the toy stands about 12 inches high, 8 inches wide, and about 10 inches long (FIGS. 6-1 and 6-3). Study the ingenious all-wood construction and see how the toy is jointed and put together. The toy has no messy or potentially dangerous nails, pins or

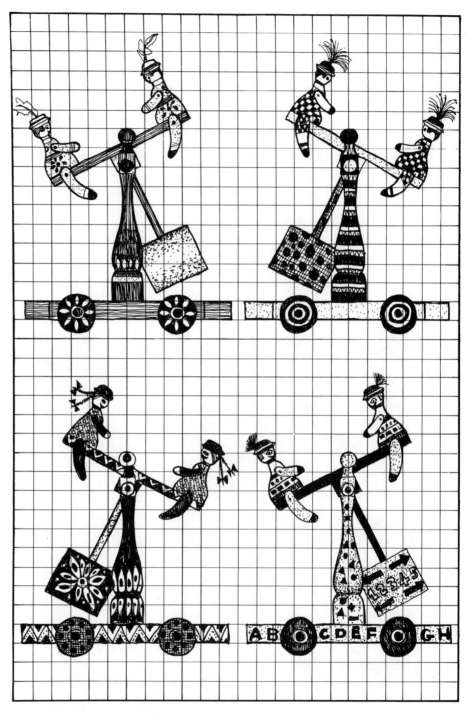

Fig. 6-2. Painting grid. Use strong, primary colors and make direct and bold brush strokes. Note the different hair, hat, and feather trim.

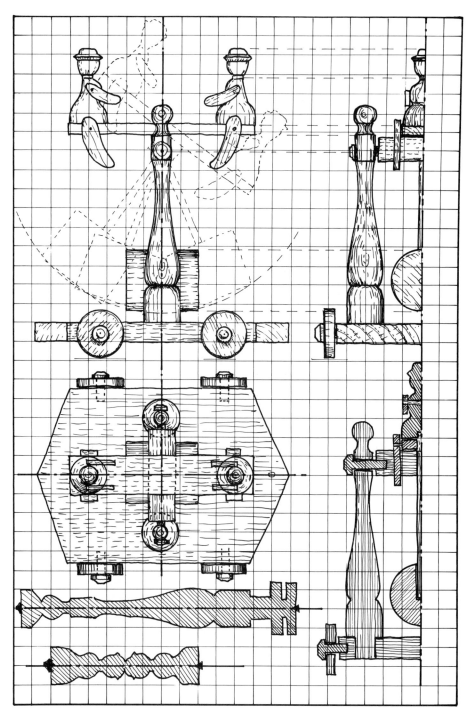

Fig. 6-3. Working drawing. At a grid scale of about three squares to 2 inches, the toy is about 12 inches high, 8 inches wide, and 10 inches long.

screws, just easy-to-make low-tech fixings like mushroom stubs for the wheels and seesaw bearings, with the whole thing held together with wooden pins.

Note especially how the pivotal pendulum mallet-shaped bob operates the swinging seesaw, and how the whole project is characterized by the use of bold design-as-you-go turnings that include two large skittle-turned forms for the main support posts, a turned cylinder for the pendulum, turned wheels, turned mushroom stubs for the wheels and the seesaw fulcrum, and turned figures. The figures are rather exciting because they relate very nicely to the German doll-making tradition of whittling a form once it has been turned (see the details and other projects).

One of the joys of working a project of this naive character is the fact that you don't have to slavishly copy every single detail. If for example you want to give the turning a miss, and shift the emphasis towards knife carving, or if you want less color, more brass fittings, bells, or whatever, then there's no reason at all why you shouldn't shape and modify the project to suit your needs (FIG. 6-2).

However, when you have considered the various design and technique options, visit a toy museum and ethnic craft shops, and get to see, touch, and study examples of traditional folk toys. Of course look at toys from India, Africa, Oceania, China, and South America, but primarily in the context of this project, focus on toys that were made in southeast East Germany between 1750 and 1920.

Finally, when you have a good understanding of just what the project involves, sit down with a pencil and workout paper, and draw up the designs to size.

TOOLS AND MATERIALS

You need ✦ A slab of wood 10½ inches long, 8 inches wide, and ¾ to 1 inch thick for the base ✦ Two pieces of wood at 2½ inches × 2½ inches square and 14 inches long for the pillars and the wheels ✦ One piece of wood 2 inches × 2 inches square and 10 inches long for the two figures ✦ A piece of wood 2½ inches × 2½ inches square and about 8 inches long for the mallet-bob ✦ Various around-the-workshop off-cuts for all the other pieces ✦ Workout paper ✦ Tracing paper ✦ Template cardboard ✦ Scissors ✦ A pencil and ruler ✦ A straight saw ✦ A coping saw ✦ Calipers ✦ The use of a workbench ✦ A small lathe ✦ A selection of wood-turning tools ✦ A pack of graded sandpapers ✦ A small hand drill ✦ A set of drill bits to include the sizes ⅛ inch, ¼ inch, ½ inch, and ⅝ inch ✦ PVA wood glue ✦ A selection of broad- and fine-point paint brushes ✦ Model maker's acrylic matte paint, colors to suit ✦ A tin of high-gloss yacht varnish ✦ All the usual workshop items like old cloths, newspapers, throw-away paint tubs, and turps.

FIRST STEPS

Take the 10½-inch-long, 8-inch-wide, ¾-inch-thick piece of prepared wood, that is the wood for the base, and mark in a center-line. Use a pencil and set-square to run a mark across the width of the wood at a point about 1¼ inch from each end. Establish the four areas of corner waste and clear them away with the small straight saw. Take the various prepared sections and scraps and cut a piece at about ¾-inch- × -¾-inch square and a little over 1½ inches long for the fulcrum bar (the bar under the seesaw) and a piece of thin slat at about 1¾ inch wide and 8 inches long for the seesaw itself.

When you come to making the limbs, take a tracing from the working drawing and carefully pencil-press transfer the traced lines through to your chosen piece of thin wood. Make sure the lines are well established, then secure the wood in the vise and set to work with the coping saw fretting out the profiles (FIG. 6-4). And so you work, holding the saw so that the blade passes through the wood at right angles to the working face, and cutting a little on the waste side of the drawn lines until the eight little limbs have been fretted out.

Finally, when you have worked the seesaw, the fulcrum block, the base, and the limbs, take the rasp and the graded sandpapers and rub the forms down to a good, smooth, round-edged finish.

TURNING THE MAIN PILLARS AND THE WHEELS

Have a look at the working drawings and see how the wheels and the main pillars can be turned from the same piece of wood (FIG. 6-3). You might,

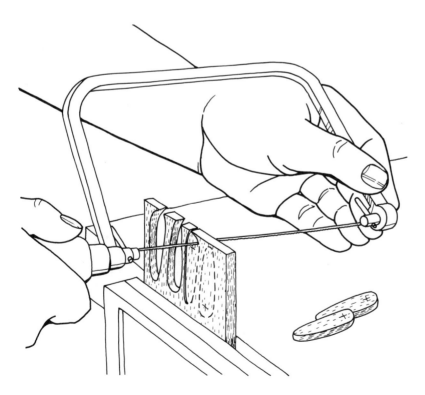

Fig. 6-4. Cutting out the limbs. Hold the coping saw so that the blade passes through the wood at right angles to the work face. Work with a steady action, all the while being ready to reposition either the saw or the wood so that the blade is always presented with the line of next cut.

for example, turn a pillar and two wheels from one length, or two pillars from one length and four wheels from another, or whatever. Consider your wood sizes and modify and work the turnings accordingly.

Draw the pillar and wheel profiles up to size. Take tracings and pencil-press transfer the traced lines through to the working face of your template card. When you have made absolutely sure that the profiles are workable, take the scissors and cut away the waste so that you are left with a negative *around-the-form* image.

Assuming that you are going to follow our way of working and turn one pillar and two wheels from the same length of wood, take your chosen 2½-inch- × -2½-inch square section and check it over to make sure that it is free from splits, twisted grain, knots, and stains. Now, with a pencil, ruler, and compass, draw diagonals on the square-cut ends, then inscribe circles that are about 2⅛-inch in diameter and draw tangents to the diagonals to make octagons. Run pencil lines from the angles of the octagons and down the length of the wood to establish the main areas of waste. Take your chosen tool—it might be a rasp, plane or drawknife—and remove the waste to achieve an octagonal section.

Make sure that the whole working environment is in good order and that you are ready, meaning that the lathe switches are working, the tools are at hand, your clothes and hair are tied back, and you have made a decision about whether or not you are going to wear a safety visor and/or a dust mask.

Mount the wood between lathe centers and set the tool rest as close as possible to the work. If you are working with a dead center in the tailstock, ease it back half a turn and oil the spin-hole. Now switch on and use the round-nosed chisel to swiftly turn the wood down to a 2⅛-inch-diameter cylinder.

When you have brought the wood to a good finish, take the cardboard template and a pencil, and working from left to right along the wood, mark in all the hollows that go to make up the design.

You need to mark in the start and finish of the finial ball (that is the ball at the top of the pillar), the hollows that occur on either side of the see-saw bearing, and so on, all the way through to the pillar spigot and the two wheels.

Take the parting tool and register the depth of the various hollows by making guide or pilot cuts. Take the tool of your choice—you might use a round-nosed chisel or a skew chisel—and turn away the waste at the hollows. Check the profile against the template. When you have what you consider is a good clean form, take the graded sandpapers and rub the work down to a smooth finish. Take the parting tool, and being careful that you don't part right off, cut in further between the waste, the pillars, and the wheels. Finally, take the wood from the lathe and complete the parting off with the straight saw.

TURNING AND WHITTLING THE TWO FIGURES

Check that the 2-inch- × -2 inch-square wood is smooth grained and free from flaws. Set out the ends with diagonals, 1½-inch-diameter circles and tangents, then remove the corner waste, set the wood securely between lathe centers and swiftly turn the wood down to a smooth 1½-inch-diameter cylinder. then remove the corner waste, set the wood securely between lathe centers and swiftly turn the wood down to a smooth 1 ½-inch-diameter cylinder.

When you have achieved a smooth-faced 1½-inch-diameter cylinder, take a pencil, ruler, and the cardboard template and mark out all the necks and hollows that go to make up the two figures. Check the marks carefully and when you are sure that all is correct, take a parting tool and cut into the required depth (FIG. 6-5). Waste the hollows using the pilot cuts and the template as a guide.

Don't be in a hurry to turn out the waste. Much better to ease it out with a series of cautious side-to-side sweeps. Working from left to right along the length of the wood, aim to establish the size and diameter of the base, the base-to-waist cone, the swelling from waist to neck, the head and the hat. When you come to the halfway mark—the point where the two figures meet head to head—reverse the template and turn off the other figure.

When you have achieved all the sweeps, dips, and curves that go to make up the two forms, take the graded sandpapers, and being careful not to overdo

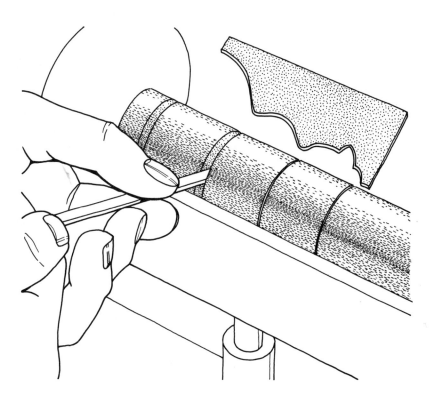

Fig. 6-5. Turning the figures. Set out the various spacings and use the parting tool to establish the depth of the hollows.

the sanding and blurr the crisp shapes, rub the wood down to a smooth finish. Remove the wood from the lathe and part off the two figures.

Have a good look at the side profile views on the working drawings and see how the figures need to be cut and whittled from waist to neck. Piece at a time, take the knife in one hand and the figure in the other (so that the head end is furthest away from you) and carefully slice away the proud curve of wood from the waist to the back of the neck. Don't try for realism, just make one or two controlled cuts to achieve a stylized figure that looks to have a straight flat back and a curved chest.

TURNING THE PENDULUM BOB

Take your chosen length of 2½-inch × 2½-inch wood, draw out diagonals, inscribe a 2¼ inch-diameter circle and cut away the bulk of the waste to leave it more or less octagonal in section. Secure the wood between lathe centers, check that the lathe is in good order, switch on, and swiftly turn the wood down to a 2¼-inch-diameter cylinder.

Take the parting tool, and with the calipers set at about 3 to 4 inches, mark off in the center the length of the mallet. Take a small gouge, hold it on its back and at right angles to the wood being worked, and turn away the two ends of waste. Working along the wood from left to right, taper in towards the bob, leaving 3 to 4 inches, and taper out. With the central area now looking as if it is pivoted between the points of two cones, take the skew chisel and work the wood to a good finish. Finally, rub the wood down and carefully part off.

TURNING THE MUSHROOM AXLE AND SEESAW STUBS

Once you have prepared your chosen length of wood for the lathe (as already described in previous sections), secure it between centers and make sure that the calipers and templates are at hand. Turn the six little mushrooms in much the same way as the figures, only this time keep checking the work with the template to ensure uniformity. Part off with the straight saw and bring the cut faces of all six stubs to a good finish with the sandpaper.

PUTTING TOGETHER

When you have worked and turned all the pieces that go to make up the toy, set them out on the workbench and refresh your eye by having a good long look at the various working drawings and details. Along the way, spend time whittling 20 or more hard-wood fixing pins—pins that are octagonal in section and a tight fit in a ⅛-inch-diameter hole.

Take the four pieces that go to make up the counterbalance pendulum, the bob, the shaft, the fulcrum block, and the seesaw, and carefully mark out the position of the various holes. Bore a ½-inch-diameter hole in the mallet-shaped pendulum bob, on the underside of the fulcrum block, and at the pivotal points at each end of the fulcrum block.

Fig. 6-6. Putting together. Drill, fix, and peg the shaft. Peg the see-saw plank to the fulcrum block.

Fig. 6-7. Putting together. Trim away a slice of wood from the back of each figure and fix with glue and pegs.

Fit the bob to the shaft, the shaft to the block, and the block to the see-saw, and bore out the ⅛-inch-diameter dowel-pin fixing holes (FIG. 6-6). Check that all is correct, then take the unit apart, dribble PVA glue on all mating surfaces, put the parts back together and hammer home the four wooden fixing pins.

In like manner, position, mark, drill, glue, and pin the two figures on the ends of the seesaw plank (FIG. 6-7). Note that the location pins on the underside of the figures needs to be larger, at about ¼ inch in diameter, and the legs need to be pinned to the seesaw rather than to the figures.

Take the slab base and bore out the two 1-inch-diameter pillar spigot holes. Now, having also drilled a ½-inch-diameter hole through the top of each pillar, tap the pivotal mushroom stubs through the pillar holes, locate the fulcrum block, push the pillar spigots in the base, and fit-and-fix with glue and wooden pins (FIG. 6-8).

Finally, mark and drill the stub axle holes in the base and the wheels, dab glue on the ends of the mushroom axle stubs, push them through the loose-fit wheel holes, and tap them home.

PAINTING AND FINISHING

When the glue is set, clean up all the dust and debris, retreat to the area that you have set aside for painting, set out your brushes and a range of good strong bold primary and secondary colors, and have another look at how

Fig. 6-8. Putting together. Peg and fix the two pillars and locate the pillar spigots in the base holes. If all is well, the see-saw should be an easy swinging fit.

the project might be painted (FIG. 6-2). Lay on a generous coat of white primer and an undercoat, not forgetting to let the paint dry out between coats. When the undercoat is dry, have a swift rub down to remove any blobs or dribbles.

Lay on the acrylic colors starting with the largest blocks. Bear in mind that acrylics become touch-dry in about 15 minutes. You might paint the base and the seesaw green, the pillars yellow, the figures and wheels red, and so on. When the ground colors are dry, take a fine-point brush and pick out all the patterns and motifs that go to make up the design (the flower petals round the wheels, the pillars and the ends of the mallet bob, the hair, eyes and mouth, the flowers on the figures, and so on).

Finally, lay on a generous coat of high-shine yacht varnish, drill and fix the hat feather and the pull-rope, and the toy is finished.

HINTS

When you are choosing your wood, go for an easy-to-turn, close-grained, knot-free variety, like apple, cherry, or sycamore.

If you do decide to use metal fixings rather than wooden pins, make sure that they are made of brass.

We have chosen to use acrylics rather than model maker's enamel paints because of the acrylics' swift drying time.

It's most important because this toy is going to be used by a toy-sucking toddler, that all the materials are safe. The wood needs to be splinter resistant and nontoxic. The paints must be nontoxic, and wherever possible, sharp edges and corners must be rubbed down.

Making a Set of
Soldier Skittles

Fig. 7-1. The full set of ten
skittles. Note how, by
counterchanging the colors, it is
possible to achieve two exciting
uniform types.

KNOWN VARIOUSLY AROUND THE WORLD AS BOWLS, *SKITTLE-ALLEY*, *SKIT-tle-ball*, fivepins, ninepins, tenpins, pinball, quilles, kegelspiel, kales, the game of *skittles* is one in which the player tries to knock over as many skittles, blocks or ninepins as possible by rolling a wooden ball at them. In England there has always been a close link between bowling alleys or skittle alleys and pub drinking, so much so that a free and easy rather carefree life of eating, drinking, and making merry is now commonly described as "all beer and skittles."

From age to age the game has been banned on account that it was dangerous, immoral, in competition to archery, time wasting, and so on. As to the origins of the game, it's so very old that really it is impossible to say for certain when and where it was first played. Enough to know that there were sets of skittles or ninepins in ancient Egypt, in Greece, in Rome, in medieval Europe, and in Victorian England.

Old German accounts suggest that the game started as a religious ritual, one in which the pins represented the devil and the ball the power of God. The game was thought of as being a contest between good and evil with the player being on the side of good and trying his level best to knock over the devil.

When was the game first played in America? Although we know that the game of *lawn bowls* or *skittles* was taken to the New World by the Pilgrim fathers, it wasn't until about 1840 that *bowling*, or the *game of bowls*, really took off. So why in America is the game now played with ten pins rather than nine? Well, the answer is beautifully simple.

In 1842 when the American economy began to suffer as a direct result of the great bowling craze and when consequentially laws were past specifically banning the playing of ninepins, the players, not to be beaten, added another skittle or pin, called the game *tenpins* and just carried on playing!

CONSIDERING THE PROJECT

Traditionally skittle shapes are many and varied. Smooth-formed champagne bottle types are seen in most modern big-city tenpin bowling alleys. Large rather crude cider bottle shapes are seen in many rural areas of England and Wales. There are bell-shaped ninepins, there are rounded dumpy keg-shaped skittles, and so I could continue.

The thing that nearly all these skittles and pins have in common is their overall form or profile and the way they are made. That is to say they are all more or less figure shaped with a head, neck, waist, belly, and foot. And they are nearly always turned on the lathe.

Have a good look at the working drawings and illustrations. See how this project relate, not so much to modern tenpins as might be seen in a bowling alley, but rather to the more decorative forms that our grandparents and great grandparents knew as *captain* or *soldier* skittles (skittles of the Victorian drawing room or garden party type) (FIGS. 7-1 through 7-3).

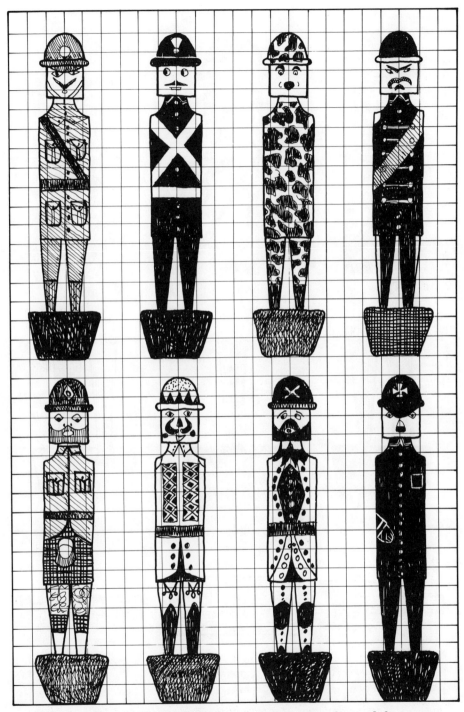

Fig. 7-2. Painting grid. By chopping and changing the colors and the imagery, it is possible to achieve all manner of exciting costume effects.

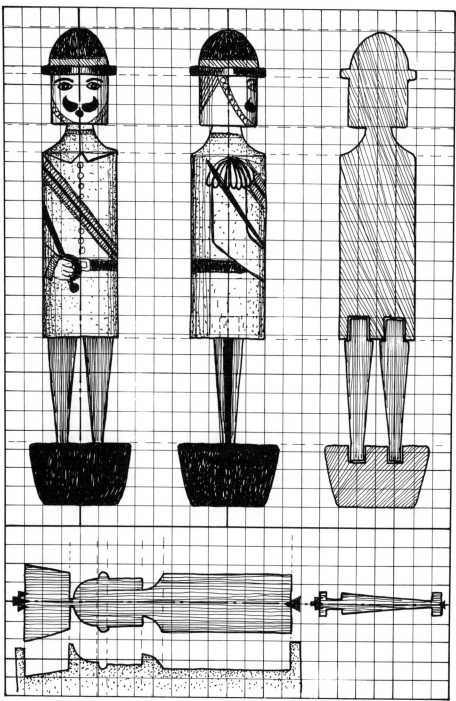

Fig. 7-3. Working drawing. At a scale of two grid squares to 1 inch, the skittles stand about 12½ inches high. Note how the legs fit into base and body holes.

This project specifically draws its inspiration from a set of soldier skittles or *military* tenpins that were made and patented in America in 1885. As to where the American skittle maker drew his inspiration, there is something about the hat, the moustache, the epaulettes, and the overall imagery of these skittles that points towards Germany. Certainly, the skittles were without doubt lathe turned in America, but probably by a Pennsylvanian German.

These skittles are special because rather than being turned all in one piece—that is with the legs being whittled out of the main turning—they are made up from four separate turnings, the head and body, each leg, and the base. See how the spigoted legs link the body to the base. As to precisely how the various parts ought best to be turned and put together, it really depends on the size of your lathe and the number of skittles that you want to make.

Of course by their very nature you need to make at least nine, but having said that, it's really a question of how you would like to work the project. For example, you could make the base blocks en masse and turn them all from the same length of wood. You could whittle the legs from shop bought dowel rather than turn them on the lathe. You could use a special chuck rather than work between centers. And so on. There are any number of ways of achieving more or less identical skittle forms. However, see how we have chosen to turn the little spigoted legs and to have the head and body and base all turned off from the same piece of wood.

Have a look at the painting grid and see how it is possible to work all manner of exciting personalized imagery just by changing colors and altering small details. Paint an upturned moustache and have the uniform a dull yellow-brown and you have a modern soldier. Use plenty of bright blue paint and a different arrangement of buttons and belts and you have an American Civil War soldier. With a little bit of research you will be able to make a set of skittles to be proud of. Finally, see how at a scale of two grid squares to 1 inch, the soldier stands about 12½ inches high with a body diameter of 2 inches.

TOOLS AND MATERIALS

You need ✦ A length of easy-to-turn close-grained, dense, knot-free wood at 2½ inches square and 9½ long, one piece for each skittle that you want to make ✦ A piece of wood at 1 inch square and 5 inches long for each of the legs ✦ Workout paper ✦ Tracing paper ✦ Template cardboard ✦ Pencils and a ruler ✦ Scissors ✦ Calipers ✦ A pair of compasses ✦ The use of a workbench and vise ✦ A rasp ✦ The use of a small wood-turning lathe ✦ A set of wood-turning tools ✦ A pack of graded sandpapers ✦ A hand drill ✦ Two drill bits, one at ½-inch diameter and the other at ⅜-inch ✦ White PVA wood glue ✦ A selection of broad- and fine-point brushes (best if they are long- and soft-haired) ✦ A quantity of white primer ✦ A good selection of model maker's gloss enamel paints, colors to suit ✦ A tin of varnish ✦ All the usual items like cloths, throw-away paints tubs, turps, and newspaper

DRAWING UP THE DESIGN
AND MAKING THE TEMPLATES

Sit down with a pencil and workout paper and start either to transfer our designs direct or to modify them to suit your own needs. Select an overall base-to-hat height, fix diameter measurements, research and draw out the details of the soldier's uniforms, choose your colors and draw the designs up to full size (FIG. 7-4).

Trace off the soldier's profile, that is the outline of the main hat-and-body turning, and pencil-press transfer the traced lines through to the working face of the template card. Make sure that the profile is to your liking and workable, then take the scissors and cut away the waste.

Finally, check the template by using it as a stencil (pencil around the card form to create a drawn image). If you have doubts about the size and details, then now's the time to sort out any problems.

TURNING OFF THE MAIN HEAD-AND-BODY FORM

As with all the other turning projects it's important that you make sure that the lathe is in good order. For safety sake it's vital that you make sure the circuit breaker switch is working, the tool rest is clear of the live head, your clothes and hair are tied back, and so on, for a pre-switch on checklist. (See the Glossary under *Lathe - safety precautions.*)

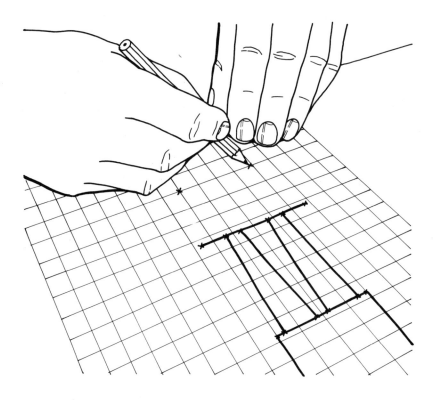

Fig. 7-4. Drawing up the design and making the templates. Use a grid to draw the design out to full size.

Start by drawing diagonals on the square-cut ends of the 2½-inch square, 9½-inch-long wood, rasp back the corners and then mount the wood securely between lathe centers. Set the tool rest as close as possible to the work, then take the tool of your choice and swiftly turn the wood down to a smooth 2¼-inch-diameter cylinder.

When you have brought the wood to a good finish, take the cardboard template and—working from left to right along the turning—mark in the position of the various convex and concave curves that go to make up the design. From left to right you need to mark off the width of the base block, the distance from the top of the hat to its brim, from the hat brim to the chin, from the chin to the shoulders, and lastly from the shoulders to the bottom of the body or coat. Take the parting tool and make a pilot cut in each of the hollows to register depth; this needs to be done between the hat and the base block, and either side of the hat brim (FIG. 7-5).

Now take the tool of your choice—you might use a round-nosed chisel or a skew chisel—and start to cut away the waste at the hollows. Working little by little and stopping the lathe every now and again to check the wood off against the template, continue until you have achieved what you consider is a good cleanly worked form. Rub the wood down with the graded sandpapers to a smooth to the touch finish. Don't blur the crisp profiles. Settle for removing all the rough end-grain patches.

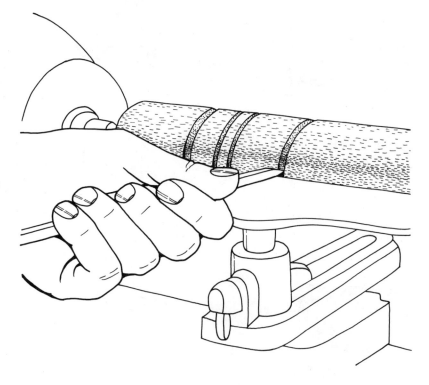

Fig. 7-5. Turning off the main head-and-body form. Take the parting tool and mark out each of the hollows.

Take the parting tool and—being very careful that you don't part right off so that the wood flies off the lathe—cut in a little further between the hat and the base. Remove the wood from the lathe and complete the parting off with the saw.

TURNING THE LEGS

Take the 1-inch-square wood one piece at a time and establish the end centers with crossed diagonals and mount it between lathe centers. Bring the T-rest up to the work and turn the wood down to a smooth ¾-inch-diameter cylinder.

Work from left to right along the wood and allow for end wastage. Cut in the ½-inch-diameter spigot, the broad end of the leg at about ¾ inch, the leg taper, and the ⅜-inch-diameter ankle (FIG. 7-6).

Check the leg for fit with both the template and the calipers, then part off. Make two legs for each skittle. And so you continue turning off bodies, legs, and base blocks, until you have sufficient parts for a set of skittles.

PUTTING TOGETHER

Clear away all the lathe waste and set your turnings, tools, and materials out on the workbench. Now, with a pencil and a straight edge, draw diameter

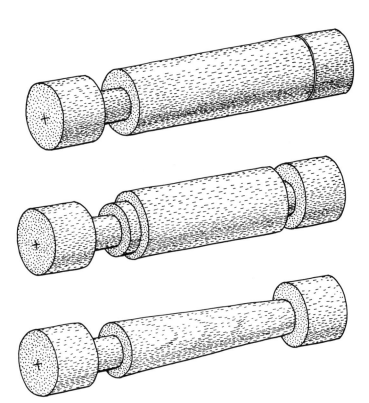

Fig. 7-6. Turning the legs. Cut-in the ½-inch-diameter spigot at the broad end of the leg and taper the ankle down to ⅜ inch.

lines on the underside of each of the bodies and on the topside, or wide face, of each of the base blocks. Fix the compass at ½-inch radius, set the point on the center of the base block and strike off a 1-inch-diameter circle. Repeat this procedure on the underside of the body.

Mark and center-punch on the base blocks and the body the points at which the arc of the 1-inch circle passes through the diameter line. Set the ½-inch-diameter bit in the hand drill and with the bit centered on the center-punch marks on the underside of the body, drill out the two leg spigot holes (FIG. 7-7). Repeat this procedure on the base block, only this time use the ⅜-inch drill bit.

When you have achieved two holes in the body and two holes in the base, take two well-matched legs and have a trial fitting. Slide the spigots in the body holes and the tapered ankles in the base block. If by chance a leg end is too tight, don't try and force it into its hole; take a sharp knife and sandpaper and trim it down to a good fit.

Finally, when you have matched up all the parts that go to make up the set of skittles, take the PVA wood glue, and working one skittle at a time, glue, fit, and fix. It's a good idea to make a couple of extra skittles, they can be used as color and design tryouts, or simply as spares.

PAINTING AND FINISHING

When the glue is dry, clear away all the dust and debris and set the skittles out in a row. Organize your working area, your paints and brushes, then stop awhile and have another look at out painting ideas and look at any oth-

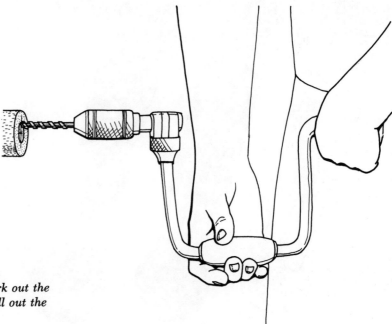

Fig. 7-7. Putting together. Mark out the undersides with circles and drill out the two leg spigot holes.

er inspirational designs that you might have collected along the way (FIG. 7-2). Consider how, for best effect, you need to use bold blocks of primary color and simple costume details. Plan out the order of painting and mix your chosen colors.

Lay on a primer and an undercoat (FIG. 7-8) with adequate drying intervals. When the undercoat is dry, work the various blocks of ground color according to their size. For example, if painting the jacket, trousers, hat, and base, you might paint the jacket scarlet, the trousers blue, the hat and the base black, and so on. Lay on the blocks of color and let them dry. Work up from the ground colors and start applying the details—the hat band, the eyes, the moustache, the sword and the belt. Continue laying on a color, letting it dry, and overlaying another color until the job is done.

Finally, when you consider the skittles well painted, sign and date the bases. Give them a coat of varnish and put them to one side to dry out.

HINTS

You might simplify the project and turn the skittle all of a piece. You could either paint in the leg divide or cut it away with a knife and saw.

If you would like to produce the skittles en masse, you could work out a way of applying the details with a stencil. You could make the stencil plates from flexible clear-plastic low-contact adhesive film.

If you want to complete the game by making a set of wooden balls, see the skipping rope project for details.

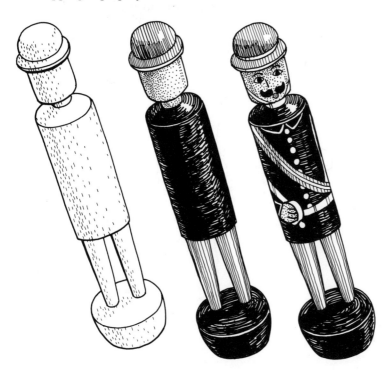

Fig. 7-8. Painting. (left to right) Lay on a primer and undercoat. Block in the main ground or base colors. Pick out the fine details.

Rather than turning the legs between centers, you could hold them in special jaws or a collet lathe chuck.

If you want to number the skittles, use rub-on numbers used by designers and sign writers. Apply them on the base just before the final varnishing.

If you only have a small power-tool lathe, you might adjust the scale and make a set of half-size skittles.

Making a Jointed Snake

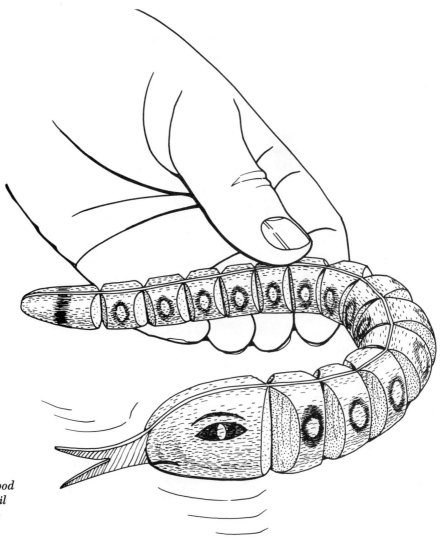

Fig. 8-1. In use, the flexible leather and wood snake is held by the tail so that the head sways from side to side.

CHILDREN LIKE CREEPY CRAWLY CREATURES SUCH AS FROGS, TOADS, WORMS, lizards, and of course snakes. With some kids the very sight of a snake is enough to set them off laughing and giggling. Most children are a bit wary about touching live snakes, but a toy—an articulated *trick* that can be pulled out of a pocket and dropped wriggling and squiggling into mum's lap—is something again! Our easy-to-make friend is a real beauty, inspired by Japanese and Chinese paper and rubber articulated snakes. He will delight children and adults alike (FIG. 8-1).

CONSIDERING THE PROJECT

Have a look at the working drawings, designs and details, and see how the articulated movement is achieved. The body is made up of a three-layer wood-leather-wood sandwich, with the wood veed or wedge cut, painted, and waxed (FIG. 8-3). When the snake is held by the tail (the 1-inch width of the strap running from the belly to back through the thickness of the snake) the slightest twist or tilt results in a truly realistic side-to-side swaying of the body.

See the working drawing and note how, at a grid scale of four squares to 1 inch, the snake measures 6 inches long from nose to tail, and about ½ to ¾ inch in diameter across the widest part of the body (FIG. 8-3). Not counting the head and the tail, there are 13 body pieces and 14 V-cuts. We have chosen an easy-to-work arrangement with the body segments ¼ inch wide and the V-cuts at ⅛ inch, but you may increase the number of cuts or whatever. The thinner the leather and the greater the number of cuts, the more realistic the movement. Bear in mind that it's best to have as many cuts as possible and note how important it is that you remove the V pieces without damaging the leather. It might be wise to make a leather and wood trial piece and have some workouts.

Finally, see if you can improve upon our design. Perhaps you could draw inspiration from various Japanese and Chinese articulated snakes that are currently being sold in ethnic craft shops; make sketches and color notes (FIG. 8-2).

TOOLS AND MATERIALS

You need ✦ A piece of easy-to-carve wood at 1 inch × 1 inch square and 6 inches long, best if it has an interesting streaky dark-and-light grain, you might use a wood like rosewood, zebrano, or kingwood ✦ Workout paper ✦ Tracing paper ✦ A pencil ✦ A thin strap/strip of leather at about 1 inch wide and 7 inches long ✦ PVA glue or another wood-to-leather adhesive ✦ A G-clamp ✦ A coping saw ✦ A sharp knife ✦ A rasp ✦ A pack of graded sandpapers ✦ A small thin-bladed fine-toothed straight saw ✦ A homemade V-block, meaning a piece of scrap wood with a ¼-inch-wide V-section groove or channel cut along its length ✦ A pack of felt-tipped pens, colors to suit ✦ A quantity of clear furniture wax, best if its

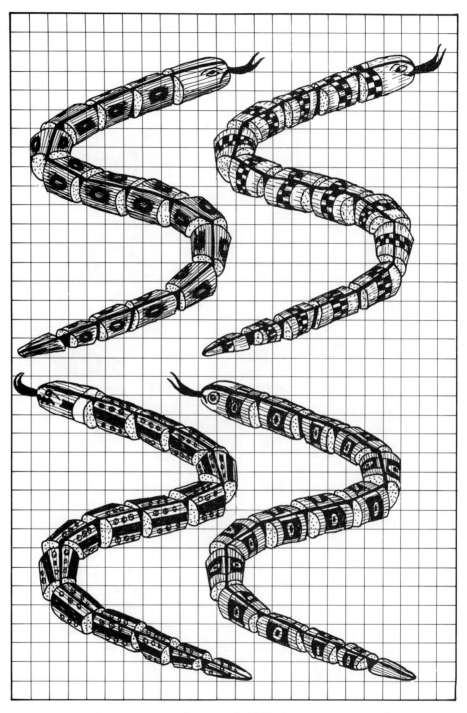

Fig. 8-2. Painting grid. Go for bold blocks of contrasting color.

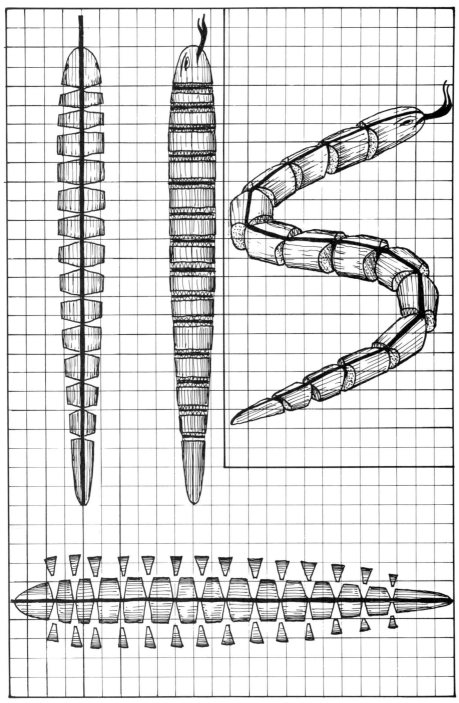

Fig. 8-3. Working drawing. At a scale of about four grid squares to 1 inch, the snake measures 6 inches long.

beeswax ✦ And you will also need odds and ends like polishing cloths, glue sticks, and off-cuts.

LAMINATING, GLUING UP, AND ROUGHING OUT

When you have considered all the tool and material implications of working this project, take the straight saw and divide the prepared 1-inch × 1-inch square section wood down its length so that you have two strips of wood at a little under ½-inch thick and 1-inch wide. With the smooth prepared faces of the wood turned inward so they are looking toward the spine, build a wood-leather-wood sandwich.

Arrange the 7-inch-long piece of leather so that 1 inch of it is hanging out at the end of the two strips of wood. Smear glue on all mating faces and clamp up (FIG. 8-4). After 24 hours or so, when the glue is dry, take a tracing from the master design. Bear in mind that the leather needs to poke out at the head end and carefully pencil-press transfer the profile through to all four long faces of the block.

Make sure that the outlines are well placed and clearly established. Use a coping saw to clear away the waste. Work through the block from back to belly, then reestablish the outline and cut through from side to side (FIG. 8-5).

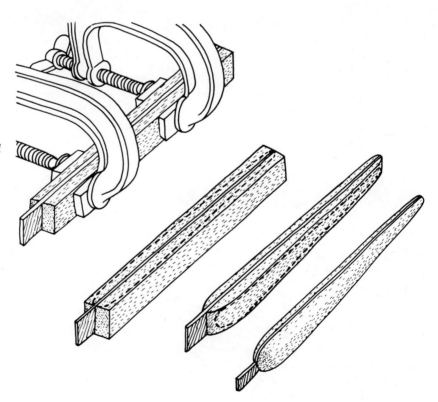

Fig. 8-4. Gluing up and roughing out. (left to right) Glue all mating surfaces and clamp up. Mark out the profile. Clear away the waste. Smooth away all hard corners and edges.

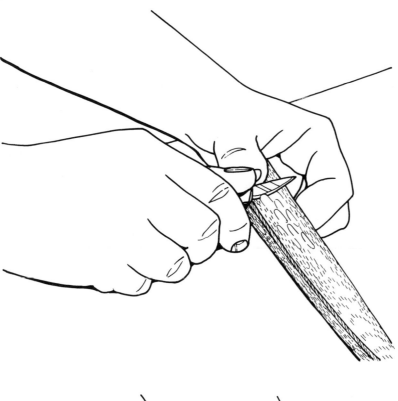

Fig. 8-5. Carving and shaping. Hold the snake by its head and remove the waste with a series of well controlled cuts.

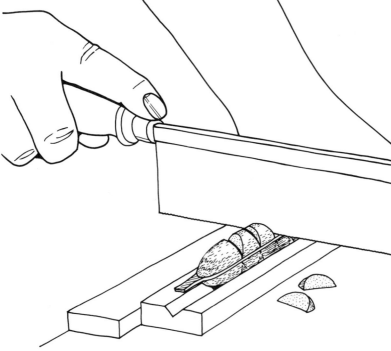

Fig. 8-6. Sawing. With the snake supported side-up on the grooved cutting block, carefully saw out the small wedges of waste.

CARVING AND SHAPING

When you have sawn away the bulk of the waste take the blank in one hand and the knife in the other and whittle away all the unwanted corners and edges. Hold the snake first by its head and then by its tail to remove the waste with a series of small, sliding, well controlled cuts. Don't attempt to rush the job by clearing the wood with great slashing strokes. Much better to remove the waste with a series of small scalloping cuts.

And so you continue maneuvering, turning, cutting, and carving until you have what you consider is a good well pulled together form. Then set to work with the rasp and the graded sandpapers and take the cigar-shaped snake to a perfect smooth finish.

SAWING THE WEDGE CUTS

Have a good look at the working drawings and see how, allowing for the head and tail, the wedge cuts are placed along the body. Use a pencil and measure to mark out the ¼-inch and ⅛-inch spacings. Mark out one side of the snake and then the other. Take the small-toothed straight saw and with the snake set side-up on the grooved cutting block, clear away the wedges of waste (FIG. 8-6). Work each V with two cuts, all the while being extra careful that you remove the whole chip without cutting the leather. Work one side of the snake, then roll him over in the groove and work the other. Finally, take a scalpel and give the snake his forked tongue.

DECORATING AND FINISHING

Clear away the small wedges of waste. Rub down all the sharp sawn edges with the fine grade sandpaper. Don't attempt to work the sawn faces, just make sure that all the sharp corners are slightly rounded. Look at the various designs and see how the patterns are drawn straight onto the smooth plain wood with felt-tip pens.

Certainly the colors do tend to run along the grain of the wood, but not to worry, because in this instance the color bleed helps to create the snaky texture (FIG. 8-2). All you do is lightly pencil in a few guidelines and then block in the color with the felt-tips. Finally, when the ink is dry, lay on a couple of generous coats of beeswax, buff the wood to a high shine and the job is done.

HINTS

You might change the order of working. Instead of cutting the V-wedges and then polishing, you could polish first and then cut the wedges. It makes the polishing that much easier and you wouldn't get wax in the V-cuts.

If you want a more sinuous snaky snake, you could perhaps give him a sheet rubber spine and increase the number of V-cuts.

When you are sawing out the V-chips, it's vital that you don't cut into the leather.

If you don't like the idea of a snake you could broaden the project and make a little *gecko* or lizardlike creature. The leather/rubber could stick out along the top of the back and be cut to form a zigzag spine.

Making a
Spinning Top

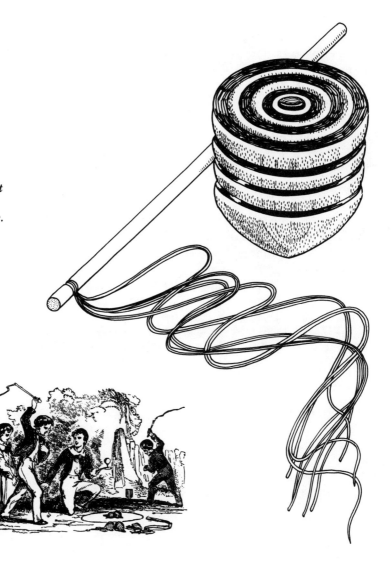

Fig. 9-1. A Victorian print showing children playing with various spinning tops.

A TOP OR *SPINNING TOP* IS A TOY HAVING A BODY THAT IS USUALLY CONICAL or pear shaped with a peg, point or metal stud at one or both ends on which it is made to whirl and spin. Known variously by the ancient Greeks and Romans as *bembles*, *stoblos* and *turbos*, by the New Zealand Maoris as a *potakas* and by the Japanese as *koma asobi* the spinning top is one of those traditional toys that was invented so long ago that it seems to have always been with us.

And like many other archetypical traditional folk toys of the same character, it didn't start out as being a child's amusement. In times past, in England, Europe, and America, playing with a top was thought of as being more a serious, social, adult activity like dancing round the Maypole, playing cricket, or square dancing. The idea was that each village had its own giant top and on high days and holidays the villagers, usually the young men could warm themselves up and get rid of their surplus energy by whipping and lashing the top around the village green.

In use, the strings of a cat-o'-nine-tails whip were moistened, wound around the top, and then with a flick of a practiced wrist it was spun into action; once spinning, the top was kept in motion by repeated lashings.

An old English adage advises family men to treat their wayward children and troublesome wives like a village spinning top. An old, cautionary, double-meaning verse or ditty that encourages this no-nonsense course of action finishes with the line: "and the faster they scourge them, the better they go." Troublesome kids, difficult wives and problem husbands be warned!

CONSIDERING THE PROJECT

Run your eyes over the designs and working drawings and see how at a grid scale of four squares to 1 inch the top measures about 3 inches high and 2½ inches wide (FIGS. 9-1 through 9-3). Note the metal nail heads on which the top spins and see the grooves running round the sides. There's no reason why you shouldn't modify the shape and make it flatter, wider, taller, spherical, or whatever; if it spins, then it's a valid form.

With this in mind, it's well worth having a look at top collections in museums. There are Roman tops made of wood and clay, tops made from the tips of cow's horns, tops made from natural forms like shells, nuts, and gourds. There are literally hundreds of different eighteenth and nineteenth century mechanical tops—tops that are designed variously to moan, groan, hum, whistle, and sing.

Each and every age, culture, tribe, village, and ethnic group seems to have felt the need to express its individuality by making its own unique spinning top form. See how in broad terms they are all more or less the same, that is to say, they are symmetrical—designed so that they have a low center of gravity—and made on the lathe. Many ethnic tops were and still are worked from whittled gourds and such like, but generally speaking most spinning tops are turned.

Fig. 9-2. Painting grid. Aim for "moving" patterns and designs.

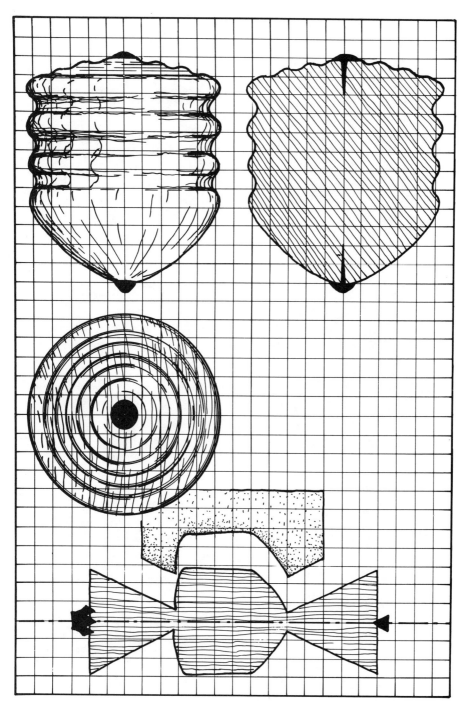

Fig. 9-3. Working drawings. At a scale of four grid squares to 1 inch, the top measures about 3 inches high and 2½ inches wide. Note the two nail heads and the use of a template.

Thousands of tops were made in the first half of this century. I well remember as a kid in the 1950s getting a little red-and-green wooden top just about every other Christmas. With this fact in mind—and knowing that it's always a good idea to start a project by trying out, or at least handling, the type of toy that you want to make—why don't you visit country sales, junk shops, auctions and local ethnic craft shops, and see if you can find a top.

When you have seen, studied, measured, and, if possible, played with a top, sit down with a pencil, compass, and workout paper and draw up your own designs to shape and size. You do of course need to make a whip. You can turn off your own whip stick or if you are a raw beginner you can settle for using a dowel, a cane, or a cut hedgerow stick.

TOOLS AND MATERIALS

You need ✦ A piece of close-grained, knot-free wood at about 3 inches × 3 inches square and 6 to 7 inches long, traditionally tops were made of boxwood and fruit wood ✦ Workout paper ✦ Tracing paper ✦ A small piece of template cardboard ✦ A pencil and measure ✦ A pair of compasses ✦ A pair of scissors ✦ A rasp ✦ A center punch ✦ The use of a small lathe ✦ A woodscrew chuck ✦ A pair of calipers ✦ A selection of wood-turning tools ✦ The use of a workbench ✦ A small straight saw ✦ A pack of graded sandpapers ✦ A couple of long, thin wood screws ✦ A selection of acrylic paints, colors to suit ✦ A tin of varnish ✦ A selection of fine-point brushes ✦ A couple of brass dome-headed upholstery tacks/nails ✦ A small hammer ✦ A cane dowel or rod at about 18 inches long ✦ A piece of cotton or linen cord at about 120 inches long

WORKING THE DESIGNS
AND CUTTING THE TEMPLATE

When you have seen as many spinning tops as possible, take your compass, measure, pencil, and workout paper, and draw the design out to size. Establish the overall height, the width at the shoulders, the conical or pear-shaped curve of the base and the decorative features (FIG. 9-3).

When you have finalized the shape of the drawn profile, trace off the design and then pencil-press transfer the traced shape through to the working face of your template card. When you have achieved a good symmetrical form, take the scissors and, working on the waste side of the pencil line, cut out the template profile (FIG. 9-4).

Check the template by using it as a stencil. Work either side of a center-line and draw around the template when it is faceup, then create the total form by repeating the procedure with the template reversed.

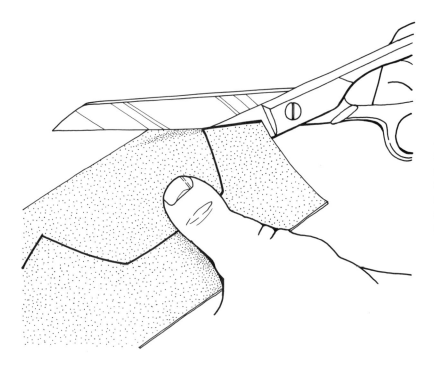

Fig. 9-4. Working the designs and cutting the template. Take the scissors and, working on the waste side of the drawn line, cut out the template profile.

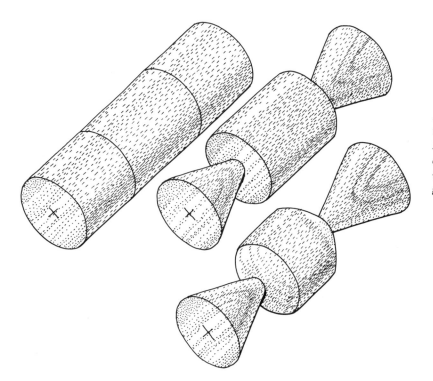

Fig. 9-5. Roughing out the form. (left to right) Mark off two lines 3 inches apart, turn away the waste, and rough out the general shape.

ROUGHING OUT THE FORM

Take your chosen length of 3-inch- × -3-inch-square wood (make sure that it is completely free from end splits, cracks, knots, stains, and grain twists), then establish the end centers by drawing crossed diagonals. Fix the compass at a radius of about 1⅜ inches and with the point centered on the crossed diagonals set each end of the wood out with a 2¾-inch-diameter circle. Now take the rasp and swiftly cut away the bulk of the waste. Don't try and cut right down to a cylindrical section, just aim to achieve a section that is more or less octagonal.

Punch in the end centers and mount the wood securely on the lathe. Run the dead center tightly into the wood, then ease off slightly and oil the tail hole so that the wood turns freely. Adjust the T-rest so that it is fractionally below center-line height and fix it so that it is just clear of the spinning wood. Make sure that the lathe is in good order, run through your pre-switch on checklist, then turn on the power.

Take the round nose chisel, make a few swift practice passes along the length of the spinning wood, then turn the work down to a smooth 2¾-inch-diameter cylinder. Take the parting tool and exactly halfway along the cylinder mark off two lines that are 3 inches apart (FIG. 9-5).

Work first from one end of the wood and then from the other to turn away the waste pieces on either end and rough out the basic spinning top shape. Work the wood as near as possible to the required profile and stop short when it is slightly oversized. Aim for a good smooth finish. Remove the wood from the lathe and part off with the straight saw.

WORKING ON THE WOOD-SCREW CHUCK

Mount the wood-screw chuck on the lathe, secure the rough spinning top on the wood screw, then wind up the dead center or tail stock. In this instance, don't tighten up the dead center as you might do when you are working between centers, but rather have it so that the point of the dead center is just touching and supporting the pointed end of the partially turned form.

Take the tool of your choice and turn off concave and convex undulations (the cord grooves that run round the top half of the pear shape) that go to make up the top half of the design (FIG. 9-6). Finish off the rippled grooves with a fold of fine-grade sandpaper.

Draw back the dead center and, being careful not to throw the spinning form off center, bring the pointed end of the pear-shaped form to a good smooth finish. When you have worked the spinning top from the shoulder line down to the point, unscrew it from the chuck and remount it point on. Being very careful that you don't throw too much weight on the side of the spinning wood, move the tool rest over the bed of the lathe and work the wood end on (FIG. 9-7). Turn off the shoulders and the decorative grooves and use a scrap of fine-grade sandpaper to bring the wood to a perfect finish.

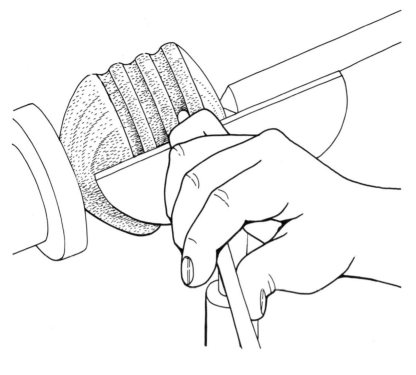

Fig. 9-6. Working on the wood-screw chuck. Turn off the convex and concave undulations.

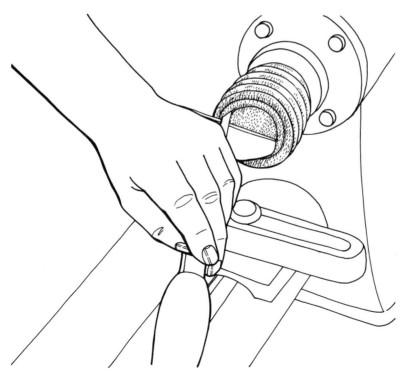

Fig. 9-7. Working on the wood-screw chuck. Turn off the shoulders and the decorative grooves.

PAINTING AND FINISHING

Remove the work from the lathe, clear away the dust and debris, and retreat to the clean dust-free area that you have organized for the painting. Set out your paints and brushes and generally make sure that all your tools and materials are comfortably at hand. Before you start painting, screw the wood screws into the ends of the spinning top so that you can maneuver it without actually touching a surface that is to be painted.

Hang the spinning top from a couple of cords or support it over the top of a cardboard box (FIG. 9-8) and lay on a primer and an undercoat with an adequate drying interval. When the undercoat is dry, select the acrylic paint of your choice and lay on a couple of base coats.

While the ground paint is drying, consider how best your chosen design might be painted (FIG. 9-2). When the ground paint is dry, lay on all the dots, dabs, lines, and daubs that go to make up your chosen design.

Lay on a couple of coats of varnish, remove the woodscrews, and tap the brass dome-headed upholstery pins in at the top and bottom.

Cut the 120 inches of cord into nine equal lengths, knot them onto the end of the whip stick and you are ready for the off.

HINTS

You could modify the project and make one of the more advanced spinning tops. Perhaps you could make a hollow top that hums or maybe one that is operated with a pull cord.

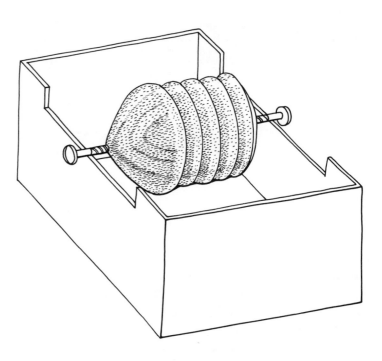

Fig. 9-8. Painting and finishing. To achieve the smooth flowing lines, support the finished spinning top over a cardboard box. Slowly rotate the form against the loaded brush.

If you don't have a wood-screw chuck, you can either settle for working between centers, or you can make your own wooden chuck. (See glossary.)

When you are choosing your wood, always make sure that you go for a type that is nontoxic. If in doubt, ask the supplier.

You can use gloss or enamel paints rather than acrylics. We have chosen to use acrylics because they dry fast.

When you are fixing the domed-headed pins, make sure that they are on center.

Making a
Jointed and Pivotal Camel

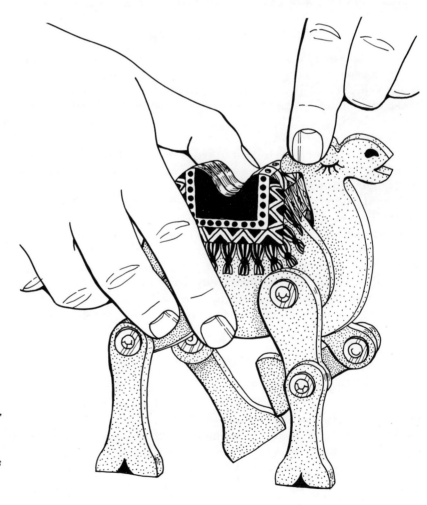

Fig. 10-1. A beautiful flatwood toy worked in the American "Crandalls" tradition. Note the pivoted neck, tail and legs, and see how the legs step out from hips to knees.

THERE WAS A TIME NOT SO LONG AGO THAT IF A CHILD WANTED A PLAY-
thing then the parents, grandparents, and the children had to get down
to work and make one. Of course it must have been a chore for some, but
many enterprising families so enjoyed their craftworks that they were able
to make a bit of extra money building and selling beautiful naive wooden
toys, such as rocking horses, dolls, pull-along animals, spinning tops, and
Arks. All wonderful traditional toys that were made with the heart as well
as the hands.

One such family, the Crandalls, who started out in about 1830 making
wooden building blocks, went on to become one of the biggest and best
toymakers in America. Their most successful toys were flatwood, painted,
articulated figures with riveted joints; figures that could stand in any position.
There were school room scenes (complete with teachers, desks, and children),
historical characters, nursery rhyme figures, policemen, cowboys, Indians,
acrobats, and zoo animals all cut out of flatwood, riveted at the joints, and
designed in such a way that they could be slotted into stands.

CONSIDERING THE PROJECT

Have a good long look at the working drawings and see how at a grid scale
of four squares to 1 inch, that is one square to ¼ inch, the camel stands about
6 inches high (FIG. 10-3). Study the working drawings and note how our
two-humped beast is worked from ¼-inch-thick multi-layer plywood, with
the neck/head, tail and legs being pivoted on soft tap-end rivets and with
the layers separated apart by washers.

Notice how our camel doesn't need a slotted stand in the Crandalls'
tradition. Because of his side-to-side thickness of nearly 2 inches he is able
to stand on his own four feet (FIG. 10-1).

Decide whether you want to copy our design or make modifications (FIG.
10-2). For example you might want to change the scale and have a larger
or smaller camel. Or you might want to go for domestic animals like a cat
or dog. Spend time working out designs, drawing up material lists, and
generally considering alternatives.

And of course if you like the overall idea of the project, but would pre-
fer to have figures or whatever, then now's the time to change the designs.
Consider all the possibilities and then draw your animal profiles out to size
(FIG. 10-4).

TOOLS AND MATERIALS

For this project you need ◆ A quantity of ¼-inch-thick multi-ply, meaning
a close-grained, white, smooth-faced plywood that is made up from thin veneer layers ◆ Workout paper ◆ Tracing paper ◆ Pencils ◆ A
workbench ◆ A V-board, sometimes called a fretsaw bird's-mouth
board ◆ A G-clamp ◆ A coping, fret, or piercing saw ◆ A small quantity
of PVA glue ◆ A hand drill with a drill bit to suit the size of your
rivets ◆ A pack of graded sandpapers ◆ A selection of acrylic paints,

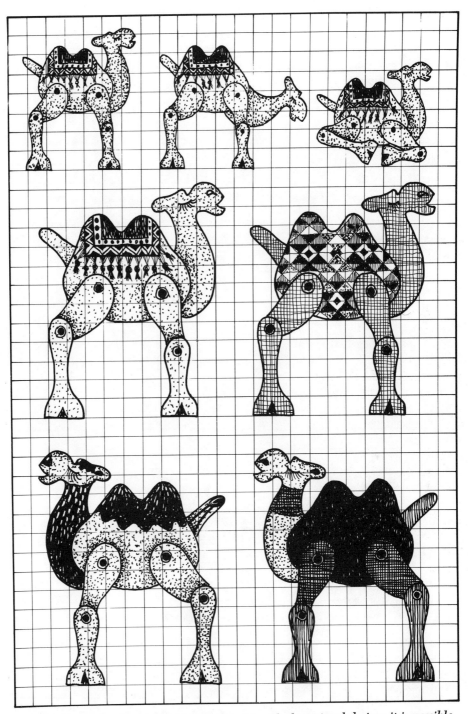

Fig. 10-2. Painting grid. By playing around with the painted designs it is possible to achieve all manner of exciting camel characters.

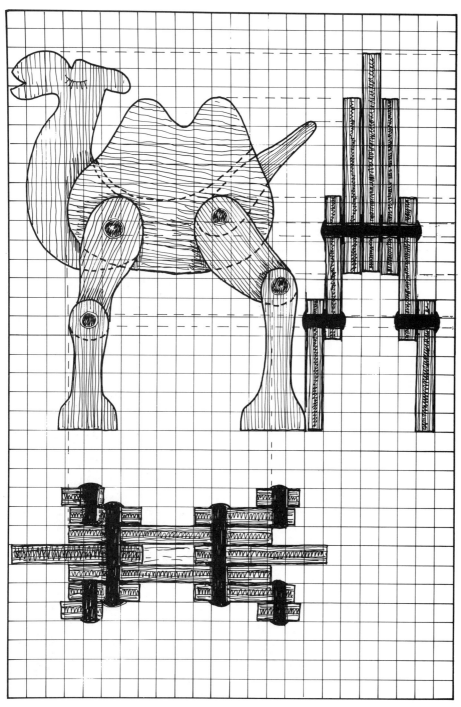

Fig. 10-3. Working drawing. At a scale of four grid squares to 1 inch, the camel stands 6 inches high and nearly 2 inches wide.

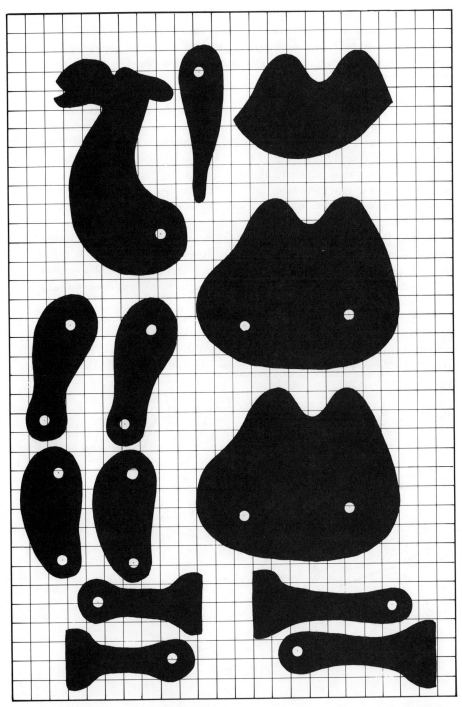

Fig. 10-4. Cutting grid. You need 13 cut-outs in all, the head, a tail, two body sides, a body spacer, and eight leg pieces.

colors to suit, best use matte, ◆ A tin of high gloss varnish ◆ Coat hanger wire ◆ pliers ◆ A selection of broad and fine-point brushes ◆ A hammer with a ball end ◆ A small piece of metal to use as a rivet anvil ◆ Six rivets, length and size to suit and 20 washers to fit the rivets

SETTING OUT THE DESIGNS AND FIRST CUTS

When you have what you consider is a good workable design take a tracing of all the parts and—with the tracing paper held secure with tabs of masking tape—carefully pencil-press transfer the traced lines through to the working face of the ¼-inch-thick plywood. Remove the tracing paper and rework the transferred lines so that there is no doubt as to the correct profile. If necessary shade in the areas that need to be cut away and label the various forms upper leg left, hump spacer, and so on.

Clamp the V-board securely to the workbench and set to work with your chosen piercing or fretwork saw. With the line of cut positioned at the V and being careful not to force or twist the saw and break the blade, work around the form, all the while making sure that the line of cut occurs a little to the waste side of the drawn line.

To avoid wood shudder or saw vibration, maneuver the wood so that the cutting line is as close as possible to the edge of the V. Work at a steady even pace with the effort-emphasis being on the down stroke (FIG. 10-5). Continue until you have cut out all the profiles that go to make the camel.

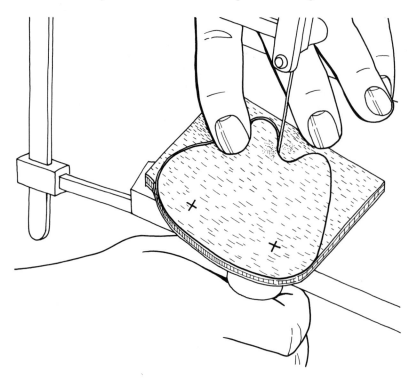

Fig. 10-5. Setting out the design and first cuts. Maneuver the wood and the saw so that the line of next cut is as near as possible to the edge of the V mouth.

GLUING, DRILLING, AND SANDING

Take the cut pieces and set them out on the bench. There should be 13 cut-outs in all—the two large body pieces, the body spacer, the head/neck, the tail, the four upper leg pieces, and the four feet. Take the two main body pieces and the hump spacer and glue stack and clamp them together to make the three-thickness hump area (FIG. 10-6, left).

When the glue is dry, establish the exact position of the various holes (the pivotal rivet holes through the body and limbs), then take the hand drill and the rivet-sized drill bit and, with the work supported on a piece of scrap wood, bore them out (FIG. 10-6, right).

When you drill the body holes, be extra careful that you don't damage the unsupported sides; slide a piece of waste between the two body layers before you drill through.

Move to the area that you have set aside for sanding and rub the wood down to a good finish. With the sandpaper mounted on a flatply off-cut (best fix it with double-sided sticky tape), continue the rubbing down until all surfaces are smooth. Clean out the drilled holes, rub off all the cut edges, and generally work away at the wood until all edges and corners are smooth, nicely profiled, rounded and completely toddler-sucking safe.

PAINTING

When all the cut-outs are absolutely smooth to the touch, clear away all the clutter and debris, make sure that the work is free from dust, and retreat

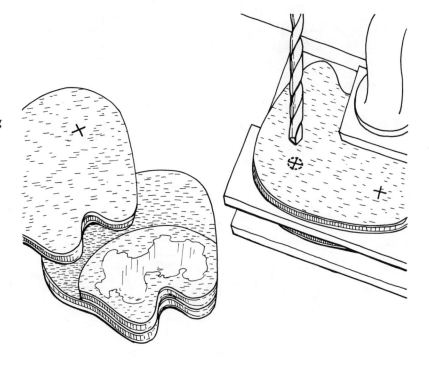

Fig. 10-6. Gluing, drilling and banding. (left) Glue the two main body pieces and the "hump". (right) When the glue is dry, support the work with a spacer/offcut, and drill out the pivot holes.

to the area that you have set aside for painting. A word before you start; it's always a good idea to check the condition of the paint, the type of brushes that you are using, the painting environment, the humidity, the temperature, or an inquisitive family pet because these are all factors that can affect the quality of the finish. The best advice is to take it slowly a step at a time. Never skimp on the sanding. Never mix different paint types. Always let the paint dry out thoroughly between coats. And best to go for several thin coats rather than a single heavy daubing.

With all these cautions in mind, spend time arranging the bodies and limbs on a drying frame or line. Lay on a primer, an undercoat, and the main ground colors.

While you are waiting for the paints to dry have another look at your inspirational painting designs (FIG. 10-2). When the paint is dry reestablish the designs by pencil-pressing the traced details of hump, face and the decorative saddle and tassels through to the painted surface. Take the fine-point brush and pick out all the motifs, patterns, and details that go to make up the design. Finally, lay on a couple of coats of varnish and let dry.

RIVETING AND PUTTING TOGETHER

Set out the painted components and be ready with the rivets, the washers, the card spacer-protector, the metal block, and the hammer. For example, when you come to the through-body pivot, have the rivet carefully supported head down on the metal plate and with the components threaded on the riv-

Fig. 10-7. Putting together. Tap the tail of the rivet over with the ball end of the hammer.

et in proper order—washer, limb, washer, body, washer, neck, washer, body, washer, leg, washer, and finally the cardboard protector. Take the round-faced hammer and tap the tail of the rivet with a dozen or so well-placed glancing blows (FIG. 10-7). Aim to carefully spread the rivet so that its tail is nicely rounded against the card spacer-protector.

When you have worked all six rivets and when you have made sure that the units are a firm stay-put fit on the rivet, tear away the card. Finally lay on a thin coat of varnish and the job is done.

HINTS

If you want to make larger or small animals, consider using a mixture of plywood thicknesses.

For example, an elephant might have the body made from ¼-inch-ply; the ears, tail and trunk made from ⅛ ply, and so on.

If you don't like the idea of using tap-end rivets, you might use pop rivets, glued dowels, or even nuts and bolts.

The joints need to be flexible but not too tight nor too loose. To this end you might consider using soft plastic or leather washers.

When you are tapping over the rivet tails, you need to support the rivet heads on a metal block. We sometimes use an old flat-iron clamped handle down in a vise. You might use the back of a spade, a piece of scrap iron from a junk yard, or whatever.

When you are buying your wood always reject wood that looks to be loose and open grained. Make sure that the wood and paint are nontoxic and see to it that all finishes are smooth.

Making a Buzz-Whirler
Noise Machine

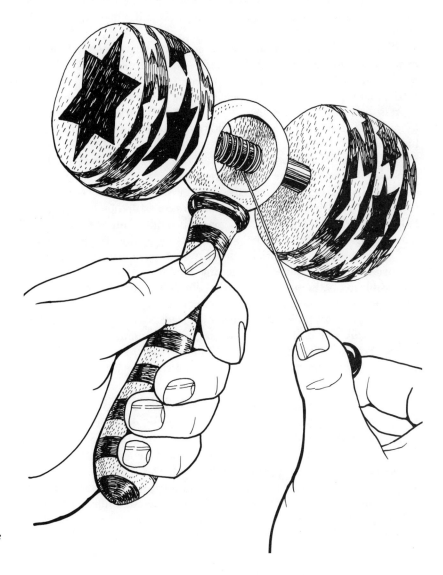

Fig. 11-1. The whirler is
held in one hand while
the cord is pulled with
the other. In action it
feels to be very much like
a yo-yo.

119

P RIMITIVE PEOPLE MADE ALL MANNER OF MUSICAL INSTRUMENTS AND NOISE machines, everything from whistles, bells, and drums, to gongs, trumpets, flutes, rattles, and of course buzz-whirlers. For noise value alone, ethnic drums and gongs take a bit of beating (sorry about the feeble joke), but when it comes to inspirational, mood-setting sound, then perhaps the most exciting are the rattles and whirlers.

In times past in primitive tribal societies, rattles, shakers, and roarers or whirlers were used, not as musical instruments in the sense that they might or might not be played as an accompaniment for singing and dancing, but rather they were thought of as being special ceremonial objects that needed to be used by the tribal shaman when he was battling against evil spirits. If a village or individual was troubled by sickness or the effect of sorcery, then a shaman, a sort of cross between a priest and a doctor, was called in to put things right.

For example, when the shaman of the Tsimshian tribe—the Indians who lived on the northwest coast of Canada—sought to rid a sick patient of a malignant spirit, one of his most important tools was a carved and painted rattle, that is a rattle that held special magic pebbles or "noisemakers." To exorcise an evil spirit the shaman would shake his rattle and he would make a slow humming while a helper would rhythmically and monotonously beat his drum.

Of course it wasn't only the so-called primitive tribal societies that used rattles in this way, village folk in places as far apart in space and time as eighteenth century America, nineteenth century England, and early twentieth century Spain, Albania, Yugoslavia, and Greece, still thought it a good idea to blow whistles, shake rattles, and generally make as much noise as possible when they wanted spiritual help or protection against the evil eye.

As to when rattles, whirlers, and roarers stopped being tools of the trade for priests and shamans, and became children's toys, it's now almost impossible to say. Enough to know that children love to make—and perhaps even need to make—a considerable amount of noise. Certainly from a parent's point of view, noisy children are, to say the least, a pain in the ear, but having said that, the sound of children at play is also uniquely beautiful.

So there you have it, if you want to make the kids a really exciting rip-roaring, whizz-buzzing, whirler noise maker, then this is the project for you.

CONSIDERING THE PROJECT

Have a good long look at the working drawings, building details and sections, and see how the buzz-whirler works in much the same way as the Yo-Yo (FIGS. 11-1, 11-2, and 11-3). That is to say, as the cord is pulled, the shaker spins, gathers momentum, rewinds the cord, and re-spins.

In use, immediately after the cord is pulled it is allowed to run slack and rewind itself back around the axle. It is the continuous action of the spinning rattle, swishing and turning backwards and forwards on its pivotal rod, that produces the curious buzzing, clicking, and roaring sound.

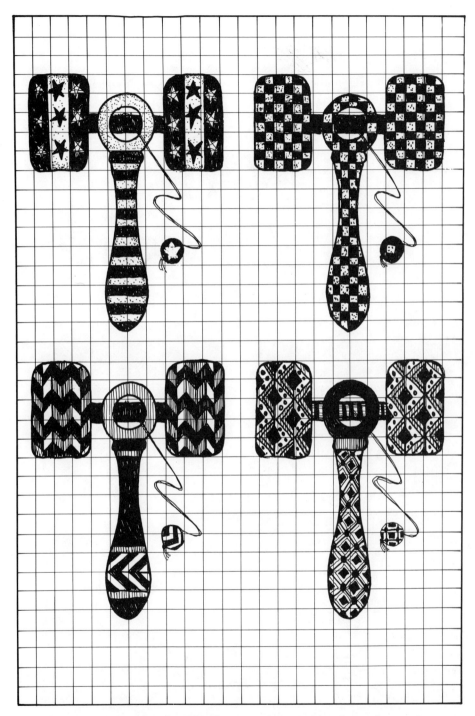

Fig. 11-2. Painting grid. Make the most of the exciting forms, best go for "moving" patterns and bright colors.

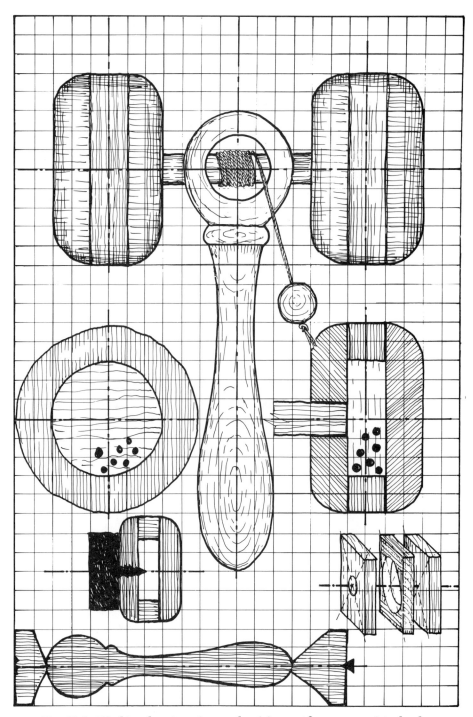

Fig. 11-3. Working drawing. At a scale of four grid squares to 1 inch, the machine is about 5½ inches wide and 6½ inches long.

See how the rattle boxes are built up prior to turning. Note how the dried seeds are popped in through the axle holes. And generally make note of how the project is put together. Consider also how this project is special because it uses and explores two wood-turning techniques; the handle is worked between centers, and the sound boxes are turned on a woodscrew chuck.

The working order is: laminate the sound boxes, turn and drill the sound boxes, turn and drill the handles, then painting and putting together. Note the working drawing scale of four grid squares to 1 inch.

Have a look at the painting ideas and see how it is possible to decorate the noise machine with all manner of exciting patterns, motifs, and designs (FIG. 11-2). As with all the other projects, it's always a good idea to have a look at similar toys in museums and collections. If possible, get to see buzzers and whirlers as made by Eskimos, the Chinese and Japanese, and by various Central and South American peoples.

Finally, when you have considered possible design modifications, sit down with a pencil and paper and draw out the designs to size. Write up a tools and materials list and generally get yourself organized.

TOOLS AND MATERIALS

You need ✦ Two pieces of easy-to-turn wood: One piece at 1¾ inches × 1¾ inches square, and 9 inches long for the handle; and another piece at 2½ inches wide, ½ inch thick, and about 18 inches long for the sound boxes. You also need ✦ A length of ⅜-inch-diameter dowel at about 3 inches long ✦ A large bead (it might be made of wood or plastic) ✦ About 24 inches of thin strong twine or yarn ✦ Workout paper ✦ Pencils ✦ Tracing paper ✦ A pair of compasses ✦ A ruler ✦ Calipers ✦ The use of a workbench and vise ✦ A set square ✦ A small straight saw ✦ A brace drill ✦ A Forstener or expansive bit to cut a hole at 1½ inches diameter ✦ Drill bits at ¾-inch, ½-inch, ⅜-inch and 1/16-inch ✦ A coping saw ✦ A pack of spare coping saw blades ✦ A quantity of PVA glue ✦ Two G-clamps ✦ A rasp ✦ The use of a small lathe ✦ A woodscrew chuck ✦ A good selection of wood-turning tools ✦ A handful of rattle noisemakers, you might use dried peas or rice ✦ A pack of graded sandpapers ✦ Primer ✦ Undercoat ✦ Acrylic paints, colors to suit ✦ A selection of brushes

GLUING UP THE SOUND BOXES

When you have drawn your designs to size, pin your drawings up around the working area and set out all your tools and materials. With the pencil, measure, and set square, take the 18-inch-long piece of ½-inch-thick wood and, allowing for end waste, mark the wood so that it is divided into six pieces at 2½ inches × 2½ inches square.

Now, a piece at a time, draw diagonals on each of the six squares to establish the center points. Set the compass at a radius of 1¼ inches and mark each of the squares with a 2½-inch-diameter circle.

With the expansive drill set at a radius of ⅞ inch, take two of the squares and clear their centers by working a 1¾-inch-hole. Now, a piece at a time, take the coping saw and—with the wood set securely in the jaws of a vise—saw well outside the drawn line and cut away the waste.

You should have six discs (or circular blanks) that are a little over 2½ inches in diameter, two of which have 1½-inch-diameter holes bored through their centers (FIG. 11-4). Arrange the blanks in two three-layer piles so that the pierced blanks are sandwiched between solid blanks.

Finally, when you are sure that all is correct and as described, take the G-clamps, smear PVA glue on the various discs that go to make up the sandwich, and clamp up.

TURNING AND DRILLING THE SOUND BOXES

Make sure that the lathe is in good order, fit the screw chuck, and set out all the tools. When the disc's glue has hardened, take the wood—a block at a time—and find the center and mount it securely on the screw chuck. Turn the wood down to a smooth 2½-inch-diameter cylinder, true the face of the cylinder, then carefully and delicately turn off the sharp leading edge to leave the work nicely rounded (FIG. 11-5.)

Reverse the cylinder on the screw chuck and turn off the opposite ends to match; do this with both boxes. When you have turned both close-ended cylinders down to small wheel or pill box forms, take the pack of graded sandpapers and rub the cylinders down to a smooth finish.

Finally, with the boxes secured flat face up on the workbench, take the drill and the ⅜-inch bit and bore out the link bar (or axle) holes—one in each sound box.

MAKING THE HANDLE

Take the 1¾-inch-square, 9-inch-long piece of wood—the piece that you have chosen for the handle—and give it a last checking over just to make sure that it is free from faults.

Draw diagonals on the squared ends to establish the end-center points, then set the compass at a radius of ¾ inch and inscribe circles of 1½ inches in diameter. Pencil in lines at right angles to the diagonals to produce an octagon at either end of the wood.

Now take the rasp and swiftly work the wood from end to end to cut away the corners and shape it into an octagonal section. Mount the wood between lathe centers, fix the T-rest in position, set out your tools, and make sure that the lathe is in good order. When you're sure that all is correct, take the tool of your choice, have a few practice runs to get the feel of the wood, then turn the wood down to a smooth 1½-inch-diameter cylinder.

Now, with the pencil, ruler, measure, and calipers, work along the cylinder marking the position of the various hollows that make up the design. Take the parting tool and make pilot cuts at the center of each hollow (cuts that register depth).

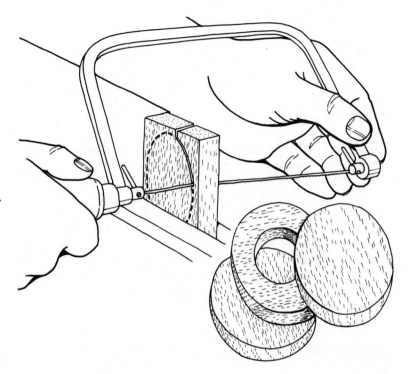

Fig. 11-4. Gluing up the sound boxes. Use the coping saw to clear away the waste.

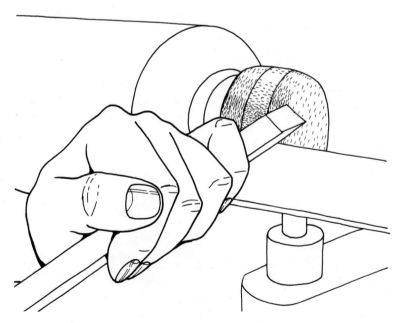

Fig. 11-5. Turning and drilling the sound boxes. Turn off the leading edge to leave the work nicely rounded.

Note that from left to right along the length of the wood cuts are necessary: between the waste and the ball-head; between the ball-head and the decorative bead or neck; at the waist; and at the point where the end of the handle meets the tail stock waste.

Now, with the tool of your choice—you might use a small round-nosed chisel or skew a chisel—work along the wood turning it down to the required profile. Although the shape of the handle can be worked to just about any design, meaning from the neck bead down to the end of the handle, it's important that the ball-head remains as large as possible. When you have achieved what you consider is a good smooth-lined form, take the graded sandpapers and rub the wood down to a smooth finish.

Now with the hand drill and the ¾-inch and ½-inch drill bits, secure the work, perhaps with a clamp and V-blocks. Pierce the ball head with two holes; one at ½-inch-diameter for the shaker box rod and one at ¾-inch-diameter for the cord. The two borings need to be worked at right angles to each other and at right angles to the axis of the turning (FIG. 11-6).

Finally, with a scalpel and a scrap of sandpaper, work the sharp edges of the holes until they are smooth and rounded.

PAINTING, PUTTING TOGETHER, AND FINISHING

Clear away all the dust, debris, and clutter, and retreat to the area that you have reserved for painting. Set out the paints and the brushes. Arrange,

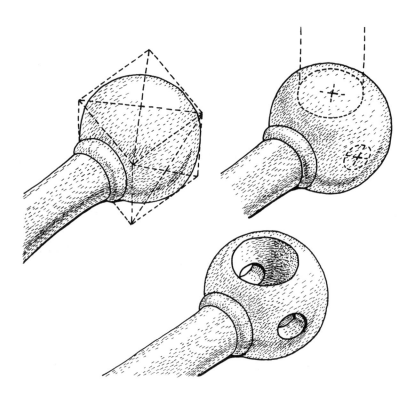

Fig. 11-6. Making the handle. Pierce the ball-head with two holes that are at right angles to each other and right angles to the axis of the turning.

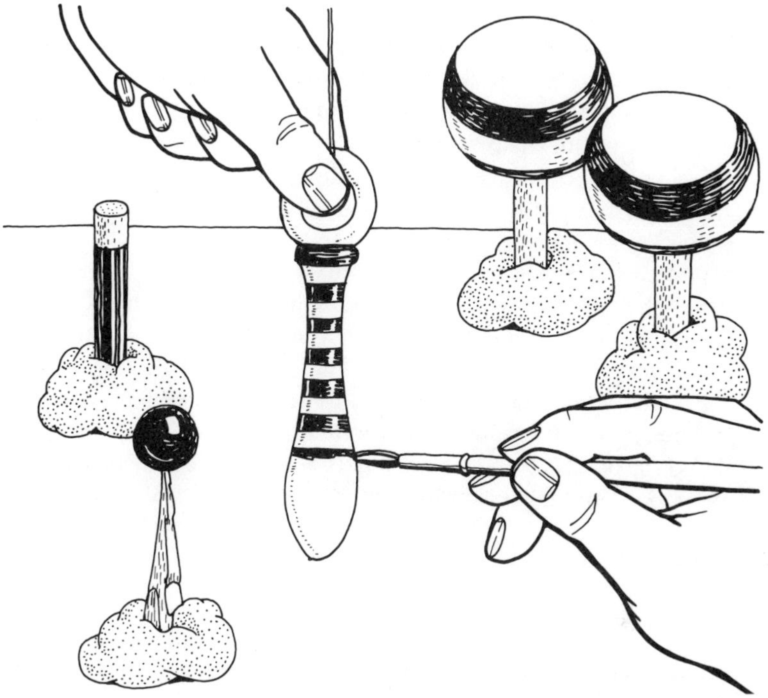

Fig. 11-7. Painting and putting together. Carefully support or suspend the five units that need to be painted.

Fig. 11-8. Finishing. Put a small pinch of dry seed in each sound box. Pierce the rod at its center with a ¹⁄₁₆ diameter hole and thread up.

support, and suspend the five units that need to be painted—the two sound boxes, the ⅜-inch-diameter pivotal rod, the handle and the bead (FIG. 11-7). Refresh your eye by having a good look at the painting design and—not forgetting that the paint needs to dry out between coats—lay on the primer, an undercoat, and the ground coat.

Wait a while for the ground color to dry, then lay on the various details that go to make up your chosen design. When the paints are dry, then comes the exciting business of putting the toy together.

Pop a small pinch of dried peas or whatever into each sound box. Pass the ⅜-inch-diameter pivotal rod through the ½-inch ball-head hole. Dab the sanded ends of the rod with PVA glue. Push the boxes onto the ends of the rod and put it to one side until the glue is dry (FIG. 11-8, top).

Finally, when you have pierced the rod at its center with a ¹⁄₁₆-inch-diameter hole and threaded and knotted the ends of the twine through the rod and the bead (you might use a needle or a piece of bent wire) the buzz-whirler noise machine is ready for action! (FIG. 11-8)

HINTS

When you are gluing and clamping the six discs that go to make up the two sound boxes, have the grain of the layers set at right angles to each other.

Use a tough, smooth twine, such as waxed linen, for the pull-cord.

There will be a chuckscrew hole on the outer face of each sound box that can be filled prior to painting.

Making a
Toddler's Pyramid

Fig. 12-1. A beautiful easy-to-make toy.

ALL TOYS HELP CHILDREN TO FIND OUT MORE ABOUT THEIR ENVIRONMENT and about themselves. Balls help develop catching and coordinating skills, building blocks enable children to use their own judgment and initiative. Skipping ropes, doll houses, bicycles, and push-trucks, they are all—in one way or other—important to a child's development.

The famous educationalist, Dr. Maria Montessori said, "Children learn by doing . . . children learn by play." And so the "play-in-school" philosophy spread, with the pyramid-type toy considered one of the best constructional or "initiative" toys for toddlers, meaning children 1 to 3 years old (FIG. 12-1).

Watch a toddler playing with the little pyramid figure and you will almost hear the child working out all the assembly combinations; should the hexagons be arranged from the largest to the smallest, could all the hexon points be matched up, perhaps the head would look better upside down, and so on.

Certainly at first sight a very young child might prefer to take the pyramid apart and chew on the pieces, but after a while he/she will find greater pleasure in sliding the hexagons on the column and arranging them to create new forms (FIG. 12-2). If you have a very young child or perhaps a grandchild, and you are looking to make a good sound "learning" toy, then this is the project for you.

CONSIDERING THE PROJECT

Have a good look at the working drawings, designs, and details, and see how this toy can be made with very basic tools and materials—saw, drill, and plywood (FIGS. 12-3 and 12-4). Certainly you do need to take the work to a smooth well-painted finish, and yes you do have to mark out the hexagons with a pencil, ruler and compass, but it really is one of the easiest projects in the book.

Have a look at the main working drawing and see how—at a scale of two grid squares to 1 inch—the pyramid figure stands about 7 inches high and is made up from a number of ¼-inch-thick plywood hexagons located on a central column (FIG. 12-3).

Consider how the units are made from one, two, or three cut-outs, with the layers being stuck together to make the various thicknesses. Worked from 12 compass-drawn circles, the hexagons are laminated to make six hexagonal units; four ½-inch-thick hexagons, one each at 6 inches, 5 inches, 4 inches, and 3 inches; a single three-layer ¾-inch-thick "head" at 2 inches, and a single layer "hat brim" at 3 inches.

The actual assembly is very straightforward because the 7-inch length of 1-inch-diameter broom handle dowel is glued into the largest hexagon. All the parts are painted with bright primary colors, while the "head" block is detailed with simple astracted features.

The project uses thin ¼-inch plywood overall, rather than different thicknesses, because it's inexpensive, easy to handle, and perhaps best of all, it can be cut with a regular saw.

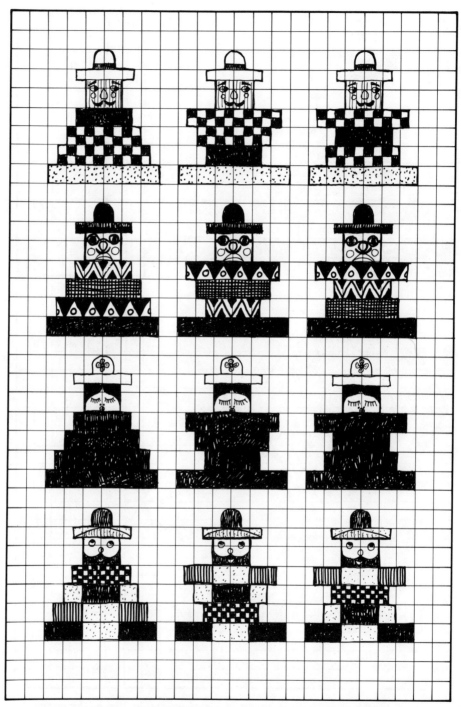

Fig. 12-2. Painting grid. It is possible to paint the figures so that there are exciting put-together variations.

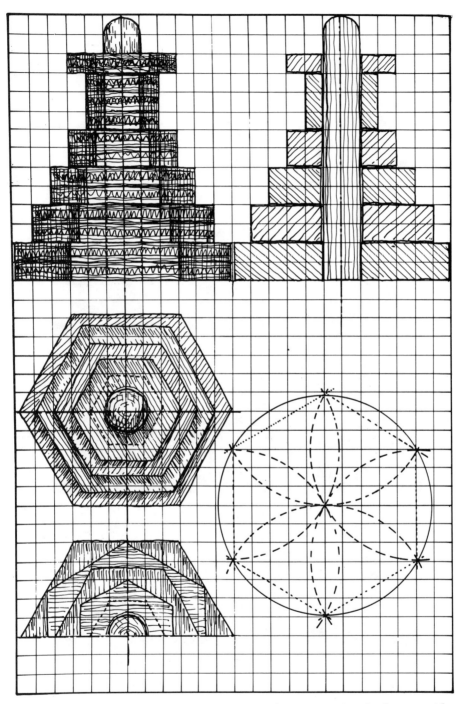

Fig. 12-3. Working drawing. At a scale of 2 grid squares to 1 inch, the pyramid is 7 inches high and 6 inches wide. Note how the hexagons are drawn using radius arcs.

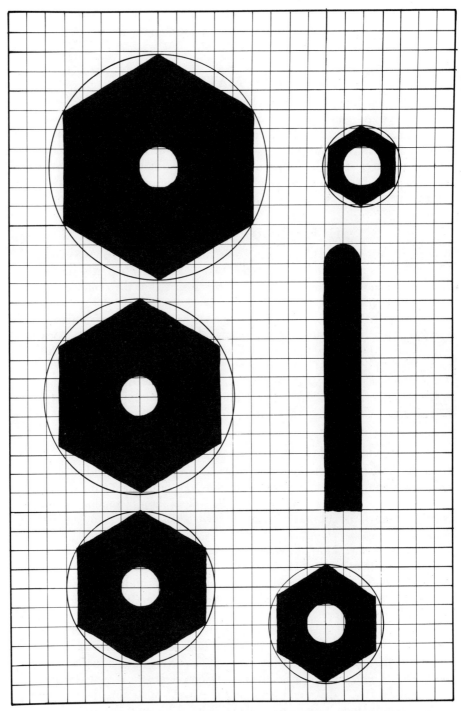

Fig. 12-4. Cut-out grid. You need a dowel and 12 cut-outs, eight for the body, three for the head, and one for the hat.

Before you decide on one or another of our designs, visit a toyshop, search out some of the beautiful plastic pyramids that are on the market, and see if you can improve upon our design.

TOOLS AND MATERIALS

You need ✦ A sheet of ¼-inch-thick plywood approximately 20 inches × 20 inches ✦ A 7-inch length of 1-inch-diameter broomstick dowel ✦ Workout paper ✦ A pair of compasses ✦ A pencil and ruler ✦ A medium-sized straight saw ✦ A brace drill with a 1-inch-diameter sawtooth bit or plug cutter ✦ PVA glue ✦ A pack of graded sandpapers ✦ Broad and fine-point brushes ✦ A tin of undercoat ✦ A selection of acrylic paints, colors to suit ✦ A tin of yacht varnish

SETTING OUT THE WOOD

With pencil, ruler, and a pair of compasses, divide the sheet of plywood into 12 circles; two at 6 inches in diameter, two at 5 inches, two at 4 inches, three at 3 inches, and three at 2 inches. Make sure that the center points are clearly marked.

Starting with one of the two 6-inch-diameter circles, set the compass to 3 inches (this being the radius of the circle) and with the point on 12 o'clock, step off around the "clock" setting out arcs at 2, 4, 6, 8, 10, and 12 (FIG. 12-3); take the ruler and join up points to make a hexagon.

And so you continue, working through all 12 circles—setting the compass to the radius, striking off arcs, and joining up points—until you have the 12 hexagons.

CUTTING, GLUING, AND DRILLING

When you have drawn out the 12 hexagons, take a straight saw and cut each shape away from the main body of wood. Now, one hexagon at a time, make six straight cuts and clear away the rough. Take a sheet of sandpaper and swiftly rub down the cut-outs until all the sawn edges are free from jags and tears.

Look at the working drawings and note the grouping of the various hexagons and then glue, stack, and clamp accordingly (FIG. 12-5). When the glue is completely dry, reestablish the center points on the six units and use the drill and the 1-inch-diameter sawtooth bit to carefully bore out the centers (FIG. 12-6, top).

The holes drilled, take the cut-outs to the area that you have set aside for the messy job of sanding—best if it's done outside in the garden or yard—and rub all the sawn and drilled faces down to a perfect smooth-to-the-touch finish. Finally, glue the 7-inch length of 1-inch dowel into the largest hexagon, wait until the glue is dry, and then sand the dowel—make sure the top end of the dowel is smooth and well-rounded (FIG. 12-6, bottom).

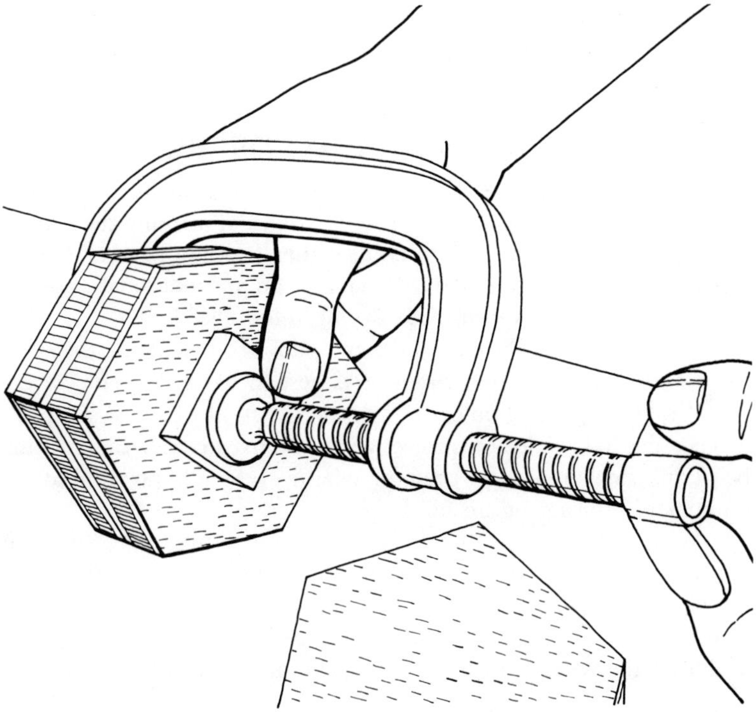

Fig. 12-5. Cutting, gluing, and drilling. Group the various cut-outs and glue and clamp-up accordingly. Note the use of scrap-wood wasters.

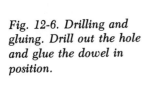

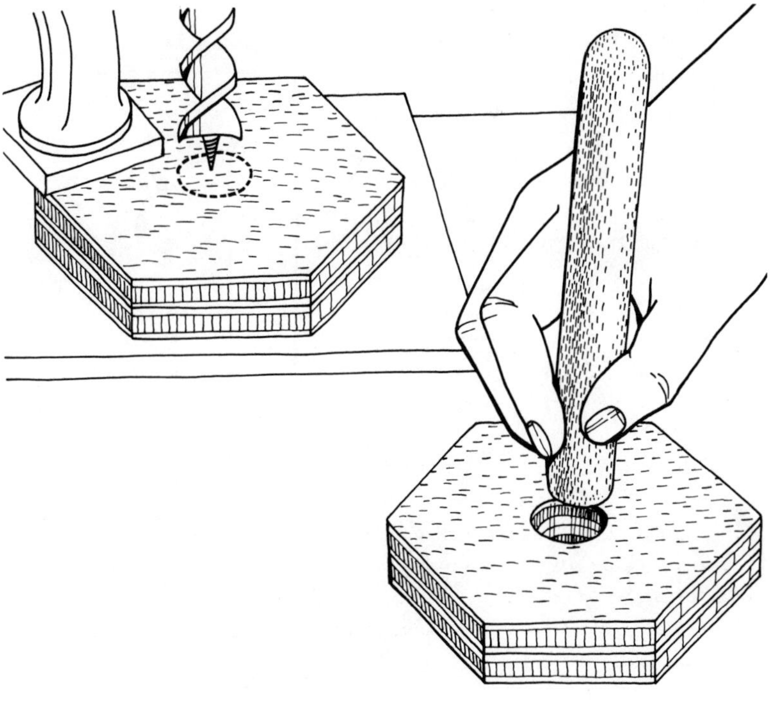

Fig. 12-6. Drilling and gluing. Drill out the hole and glue the dowel in position.

Note: Bearing in mind that the work is to be painted and the units need to be a loose fit, it might be as well to rub the dowel down to ⅞ inch and work the holes until they are about 1¹⁄₁₆ inch.

PAINTING AND FINISHING

When all the units have been worked to a good finish, meaning all edges are smooth and the hexagons are an easy loose fit around the central dowel, wipe them with a damp cloth and set them upon a rack or hang them on wires ready for painting (FIG. 12-7). Lay on an undercoat and the various ground colors with appropriate drying intervals.

You might paint the base and central dowel a bright red, the next hexagon yellow, the next blue and so on; it is best to use bold primary colors.

While the ground colors are drying, look at our designs and see how it is possible to broaden the project with patterns on the hexagons. Units might be plain, checkered, zigzagged, or whatever; it is impossible to suggest all manner of exciting figure imagery.

When you know just how you want your figure to be, take a fine-point brush and pick out all the little patterns, details, and motifs that make up the design. Finally, when you have sanded any hard blobs of paint, checked that the units are still a loose fit on the central dowel, and generally made sure that the work is in good order, lay on a coat of varnish.

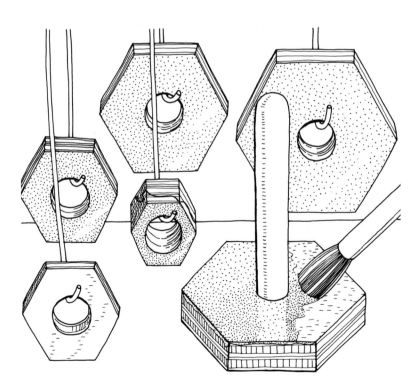

Fig. 12-7. Finishing. Hang the parts to be painted on wires.

HINTS

If you like the idea of the project, but don't want to go to the trouble of gluing up the layers, then there's no reason why you shouldn't modify the design and use ¼-inch-thick units throughout.

Because this is a young child's toy, it's vital that you use nontoxic paints. Use a sound, safe, nonsplinter plywood, such as a top grade multilayer, veneer plywood.

If you have worries about the units being too big, too small, or whatever, then follow your own intuition and redesign the project to suit your own needs.

Making a
Topsy-Turvy Doll

Fig. 13-1. The skirts conceal the other character.

FROM THE ANGLO-SAXON *TEARFLIAN*, MEANING TO TURN OR TO ROLL OVER, the term topsy-turvy has now come to describe a most beautiful double-ended type of doll. The topsy-turvy doll is characterized by having, as it were, two faces or two characters. Hold her one way up and she is happy, flip her over and she is sad. Hold her one way up and she is a little black girl, flip her over and she is white.

When and where the topsy-turvy doll first saw the light of day, who can say? Certainly there are examples of very old English Elizabethan and American Puritan *poupard* and *pestle* dolls, that is lathe turned, armless, head-and-body, wooden skittlelike dolls. And we have seen mention of nineteenth century American *Eva-Topsy* black-white double dolls. But as to when the term *topsy-turvy* first came to be used to describe such a doll, it's not possible to say.

Maybe the idea of a two-faced doll relates to various ancient customs, rituals, dances and ceremonies where sharman-dancers present a different comic-tragic character or "face" simply by wearing a different mask. Who knows? However, our "two for the price of one" topsy-turvy beauty is always capable of putting on a sad or happy face.

How is this possible? Well, like all good ideas, it's very simple, the topsy-turvy is really no more than a double ended, two-headed, two-faced, skittle-turned girl doll whose long voluminous, double layered, two-colored skirt conceals her other self. Hold her one way up and her sad face is visible, turn her over and the skirt falls down over her sad face to reveal a face full of smiles (FIG. 13-1).

CONSIDERING THE PROJECT

The lathe-turned topsy-turvy skittle doll is a beautiful traditional toy; she's strong, she's easy to make, and she's decorative. If you have a lathe and you are looking for a simple inexpensive starter project, then this could well be the project for you (FIG. 13-1).

What could be better than to spend an hour or so making this wonderful archetypal doll and then to present it to your child or grandchild? Picture if you can the look on your granddaughter's face when she views *Topsy* for the first time!

Of course you don't have to make a happy-sad girl doll; you might prefer to make a happy-sad comical Scotsman in a long droopy kilt, a happy-happy girl with a school uniform and a party dress, or a black-white lady in historical costume. There are any number of exciting and easy-to-make possibilities (FIG. 13-2).

Look at the working drawing and the various details and see how, at a grid scale of four squares to 1 inch, Topsy measures about 1½ inches diameter and 6 to 7 inches long (FIG. 13-3). Note also the simple form, the ball-turned head, and the various hollows and curves.

As with all the other projects, don't be tempted to rush straight into your workshop. Much better to start by visiting the local folk art center or toy

Fig. 13-2. Painting grid. By slightly altering the turning and the painted imagery it is possible to achieve any number of characters.

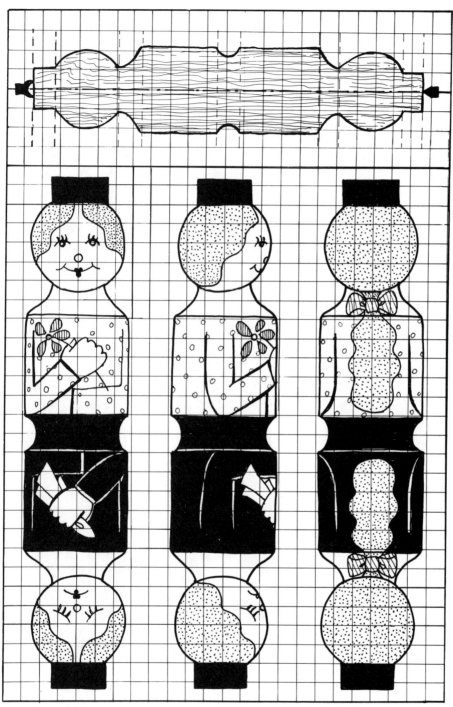

Fig. 13-3. Working drawing. At a scale of four grid squares to 1 inch, the doll is about 6¾ inches long and 1½ inches wide.

museum. View as many wooden dolls as possible. Note how they have been turned, worked and put together; see how many turned parts are used; figure out how the painted imagery might best be worked; decide how the costume has been made, and so on. Spend as much time as possible really getting to know your subject.

TOOLS AND MATERIALS

You need ✦ A piece of easy-to-turn wood at 1¾ inches × 1¾ inches square at 7 to 8 inches long, you might use lime, sycamore, or cherry ✦ The use of a small wood-turning lathe ✦ A selection of wood-turning tools ✦ A pack of graded sandpapers/glasspapers ✦ A pair of calipers ✦ A pencil and measure ✦ A selection of broad and fine-point paint brushes ✦ Wood primer and undercoat ✦ A selection of acrylic paints ✦ A small quantity of yacht varnish ✦ The use of a sewing machine ✦ A pair of scissors ✦ Two pieces of pretty, small patterned dress fabric at 30 inches long and 4 inches wide ✦ About 6 inches of plain ribbon or braid ✦ Two upholstery tacks or nails or brads, preferably made of brass ✦ A small hammer

STARTING OUT

When you have had a good look at dolls in general, and wood-turned Topsy-type dolls in particular, and once you have considered possible modifications—for example you could make a doll that is much larger or much smaller, or you might want to make a more buxom and curvaceous character—sit down with a pencil, measure, and workpaper, and draw your design out to size.

Take your chosen piece of wood and examine it for problems; avoid wood that looks to be stained, split or knotty. Make sure that the lathe is in good and safe working order, secure the wood between centers, organize the tool rest (set it as close as possible to the work and a little above lathe center height), and arrange all your tools within reach.

Switch on the lathe and use the tools of your choice to swiftly turn the wood down to about a 1½-inch-diameter cylinder. Clear away the waste and then with a chisel or similar tool, bring the wood to a good finish.

TURNING THE NECKS, CURVES, AND HOLLOWS

When you have achieved a nicely finished 1½-inch-diameter cylinder, take the measure and calipers and then, working with a pencil from left to right along the wood, mark the length of the various parts. For example, you need to establish the distance from hat to head, the length of the head from hat to neck, the length of body from neck to waist, and so on.

Once you have marked these points in with a pencil, work along the length of the spinning wood and use a skew chisel to cut-in the position of the two hats, the two necks, and the waist (FIG. 13-4). Take another good

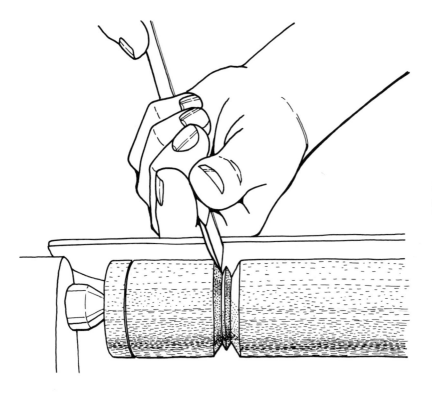

Fig. 13-4. After roughing out, mark out the various "necks" and hollows.

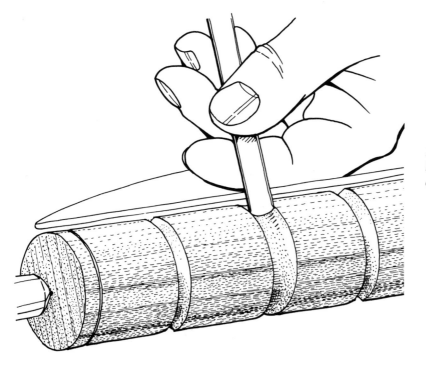

Fig. 13-5. Shape the hollows with a rolling action of the turning tool.

look at your designs, note the shape of the curves and hollows, and then take the tool of your choice and shape the required forms (FIG. 13-5).

There is no one single proper way of shaping; simply go at it slowly but confidently. If you manage to cut away the waste in smooth curls, and if the tools leave the wood looking crisp and shiny, then you won't be going far wrong.

Using the calipers and judging the shape of the curves by eye, gradually work towards a symmetrical double-ended form (FIG. 13-6). This done, take several strips of graded sandpaper and—working in the order from rough to fine—take the wood to a good smooth finish (FIG. 13-7).

Be careful as you are sanding that you don't overwork any one single area and get a blurred and shapeless profile, but rather keep the sandpaper moving to and fro along the spinning work. On large flat surfaces, say between the neck and the waist, have the sandpaper double folded and held with a cupped hand.

Finally, part the wood off from the lathe and rub the ends down to a smooth finish.

PAINTING

When you have achieved a nicely worked, well proportioned double-ended doll, clear away all the clutter, wipe the wood down with a damp cloth. Organize your painting area in one corner of the workshop that is completely free from wood dust and debris, or better still do the painting in an area that is set apart from the wood workshop.

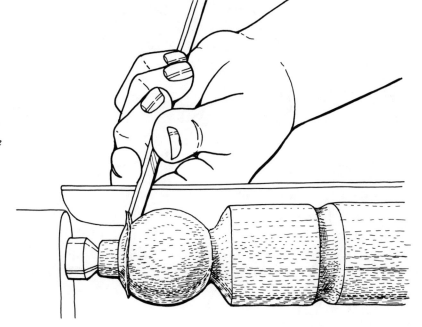

Fig. 13-6. Round off the head and cut away the waste.

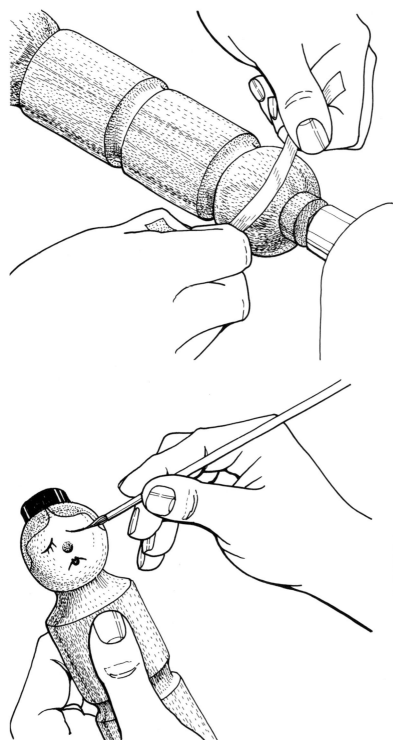

Fig. 13-7. Strengthen a strip of sandpaper with a length of sticky tape and rub the wood down to a smooth polished finish.

Fig. 13-8. Pick out the details with a fine-point brush. Bear in mind that the hat also needs to double up as feet.

Set up a drying stand or frame, or in this case you could simply paint one end of Topsy and leave her, as it were, standing on one of her two heads. Select your brushes and set out the paints. Before you start, have a good long look at your chosen dress fabrics and at the inspirational designs. See how you might work the painted imagery (FIG. 13-2).

You could stay with our happy-sad rather ladylike image and give Topsy a dark-and-light bodice to match a dark-and-light dress fabric. Or you could go for one of the other designs like a pretty polka-dot dress, and paint in a look of wide-eyed innocence. Or you might prefer an asleep-and-awake character; there are any number of possible color, pattern, and design combinations.

When you have decided on one or another of the designs, note which areas need to be painted and which need to be left in the natural wood state, then take a soft pencil and draw the design directly onto the wood. Establish and draw the edge of the hat, the line of the hair, the eyes, nose and mouth, the bodice/blouse, and so on. Select the large painted areas—the hat and the blouse—and lay on a primer and an undercoat with adequate drying intervals. Take a fine-point brush and pick out all the fine details that make up the design (FIG. 13-8).

So for example, you can paint in the hair, the bow, the design on the blouse, the flower/handkerchief, the eyes, and so forth. Continue layering and building up from the large areas of ground color until you consider the design finished.

Finally, when the paint is dry, lay on a coat of varnish and put Topsy to one side to dry out.

MAKING AND FITTING THE SKIRTS

Take the two 30-inch lengths of pretty patterned, lightweight, and fine dress fabric/material—best if you use a printed cotton—and a piece at a time turn and sew one long edge to make a ¼-inch-wide hem. You should have two pieces of material that measure 30 inches long by 3¾ inches wide.

Place and pin the two pieces of fabric so that the best sides are face-to-face, the hems are touching, and the underside or back of the fabric is outermost. Very carefully enter the long unsewn edges into the machine and sew through both pieces of fabric so that the line of stitches occurs about ½ inch in from the edge.

Open the fabric out so that the best face is uppermost, fold it in half lengthwise, and sew the ends together. You should now have a tube of fabric that is, as it were, two skirts sewn waist-to-waist. Slide Topsy into her skirts (with the fabric still inside out) and arrange them so that the waist-to-waist band fits into the turned waist groove (FIG. 13-9). Gather the skirt at the waist, wrap the piece of ribbon tightly around and fit and attach with the upholstery tacks or nails.

Finally, stand Topsy upright, straighten the skirts, and the job is done (FIG. 13-9).

Fig. 13-9. Position the skirt and pin through the waist line. Flip the skirt over to reveal one or other of the faces.

HINTS

When you select your wood, make sure that it is smooth grained and free from knots, splinters, and sappy edges.

If the wood turns up rough on the lathe, make sure that the wood is dry and resharpen the tools.

If you decide to use gloss enamel or model-makers oil paints, rather than acrylics, allow extra time for drying.

When you are sewing the hem edge you might use a decorative ribbon or braid.

Because this is primarily a toddler's toy, a toy that is likely to be cuddled, sucked, and generally held close, make sure that all the materials are safe. Use fire resistant cotton for the skirt. Make sure that the wood is splinter resistant and nontoxic. Make sure that nails are made of brass and hammered in well. And finally, perhaps most important of all, make sure that the paint is nontoxic.

If you are worried about using nails, use screws or contact adhesive.

Making a Pull-Along
"Barrel" Horse

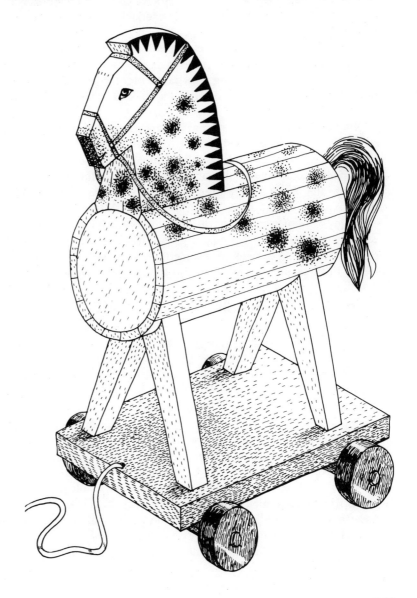

Fig. 14-1. The barrel horse is
characterized by having a
coopered body, a strong form
and bold lines.

AFTER DOLLS, SOLDIERS, NOAH'S ARKS, AND, SINCE THE SECOND WORLD WAR, cars, I think it is fair to say that of all the large prestigious toys, the *horse* is the most popular. From country to country and down over the centuries, toymakers have made and fashioned toy horses from just about every conceivable material.

There are small clay horses, horses made of bronze, hobby horses with carved and stuffed heads, ride-on bicycle horses, huge realistically carved rocking horses, horses on wheels, stuffed horses covered with real horse hide, mechanical pressed-tin horses, and so on. If the exhibits in our museums, and if numerous written accounts are anything to go on, it must have been every child's dream to own a toy horse. And of course if the horse was large enough to actually sit on, and if it could be jerked into motion, then so much the better.

From about the middle of the seventeenth century right up until the early twentieth century, children were able to "gallop" about their nurseries on all manner of rocking, bouncing, and cantering steeds; wonderfully carved and painted horses that moved on runners, rockers, springs, rollers, pulleys, and wheels.

Of all these horses—some so realistic and large that they look as if they need feeding—one of the most attractive was the *barrel pull-along* horse. Made and mass-produced in England, Europe, and America, this beautiful wooden horse had a cooper-built barrel-shaped body, a flattish slab-built head slotted into the body, four splayed legs (just like a sawhorse), and it was painted, decorated, and mounted on a wheeled stand.

The joy of a horse of this character is not so much its realism, but rather its small friendly size and its simplicity. Standing about 18 to 24 inches high with a pull-along rope, reins, and sometimes even with dowel handles, toy horses of this type are the perfect toy for toddlers who are learning to walk.

CONSIDERING THE PROJECT

Look at the various designs and working drawings and see how the barrel-shaped horse is a relatively simple, easy-to-make structure (FIGS. 14-1 through 14-4). Two discs and a number of thin battens or slats make up the coopered barrel. The head is built-up and slotted into the body. The body in turn is supported by four legs that splay out from the underside of the barrel and the whole structure sits on a wheeled slab or plank base.

See that at a grid scale of one square to 1 inch the horse measures about 23 inches high, 18 inches from nose to tail, and about 12 inches wide at the base. Study the details and sections, and note how the legs and the head spring out from, and are screwed to, the main body plank and the end discs (FIG. 14-3). Most important of all, consider how the whole project has been built up from 1-inch-thick plank wood.

Certainly we could have gone for a non-traditional approach and used several thicknesses of plywood, or even a mixture of different-size wood sections, however after spending time carefully weighing the pros and cons

Fig. 14-2. Painting grid. By changing the painted imagery it is possible to work all manner of horse types, everything from a pony to knight's steed.

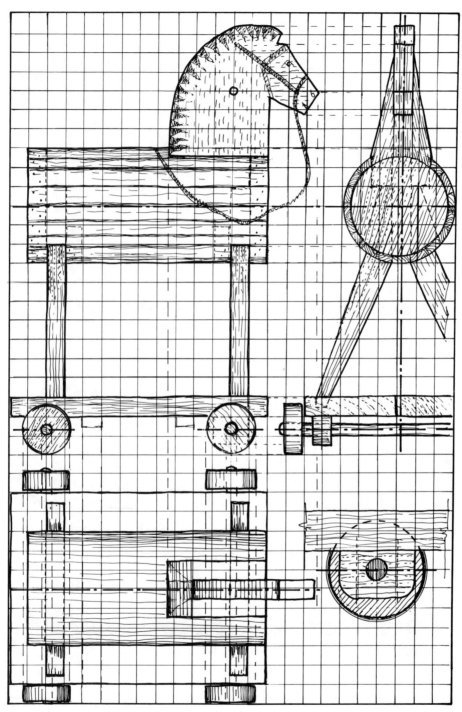

Fig. 14-3. Working drawing. At scale of one grid square to 1 inch, the horse measures about 24 inches high and 12 inches wide, a good toy for toddlers.

of the various options, we decided to use the 1-inch-thick wood throughout. There are several points in favor of working in this way: most woodyards stock 1-inch-thick wood and, perhaps most important of all, it's easier and more economical in terms of time and money if you are only dealing with the one wood size.

Before you rush out and start buying your materials, visit galleries, workshops, and museums to see as many traditional rocking and pull-along horses as possible. See how they are cut, jointed, assembled, painted, and decorated.

Finally, sit down with a pencil, measure, and workout paper and draw up your chosen design to size. List the materials, work out how the profile can best be cut from the wood, and generally spend time planning the order of work.

TOOLS AND MATERIALS

You need ✦ About 15 feet of 6-inch-wide and 1-inch-thick plank wood, best to use a good quality knot-free wood like parana pine ✦ Two ¾-inch-diameter broom sticks or dowels ✦ The use of a workbench with a vise ✦ Workout paper ✦ Tracing paper ✦ A pencil and measure ✦ A set square ✦ A pair of compasses ✦ A straight saw ✦ A coping saw ✦ A couple of G-clamps ✦ A mallet ✦ A hammer ✦ A shallow, U-section wood-carving gouge ✦ A 1-inch-wide mortise chisel ✦ A plane or a surform type rasp ✦ A screwdriver ✦ A handful of 1½-inch-long wood screws ✦ PVA wood glue ✦ A quantity of 1-inch-long oval-headed panel pins ✦ A brace with a ¾-inch diameter drill bit ✦ A drill bit to match the diameter of the wood screws ✦ A pack of graded sandpapers ✦ A small amount of resin filler, best to use a two-tube car body filler ✦ A nontoxic white wood primer ✦ A tin of undercoat ✦ Enamel paints, colors to suit ✦ A selection of broad and fine point brushes ✦ A scrap of rag or sponge ✦ A length of leather strapping or rope for the bridle and reins ✦ Material for the tail, you might use a hank of cord or somesuch ✦ Brass dome-headed upholstery pins/tacks ✦ All the usual workshop odds and ends like white spirit, throw-away paint tubs, cloth, and newspaper

BUILDING THE HEAD AND THE BODY PLANK

Draw up the master designs. Make tracings and pencil-press transfer the various drawn profiles to your chosen wood. Stop and make sure that the planned cut-outs are clear of possible flaws (FIGS. 14-3 and 14-4). For example if there are dead knots, small splits or stains on the wood, then make sure that they don't occur on visually or structurally important areas like the horse head or the legs. Cut the wood down with the straight saw and the coping saw to the component parts. There should be: the main body plank; the four pieces that go to make up the head-and-neck sandwich or lamination; the four legs; the two body discs; the four wheels; the two base planks; the

Fig. 14-4. Cut-out grid.

four axle blocks; the 20 or so 1-inch-wide ½-inch-thick barrel strips, and many useful off-cuts (FIG. 14-4).

Clear the workbench of clutter and set out the main body plank and the four cut-outs that go to make up the head. Remember that all mating faces and edges need to fit properly for the neck-to-body-plank lamination. Start by cutting, fitting, and gluing the head to the neck and the neck to the body.

Once you have made sure that the three central-core neck pieces are well glued, butted and aligned, take the two side slabs and glue and clamp them on either side of the head. Remember that the neck slabs need to be carved and angled from the line of the body to the top of the head. Secure the clamped-up sandwich with screws that occur below the body line (FIG. 14-5).

CARVING THE HEAD

When the glue is dry and set, arrange and clamp the work to the bench so that the bottom edge of the body plank is nearest to you. Wood is best cut across or at angle to the grain, so take the gouge and start cutting away the waste at the top end of the neck slab. Don't try to remove the waste with great thrusts of the gouge, but work little by little all the while removing small scoops of wood (FIG. 14-6).

Work back and forwards across and around the width of the neck to shape the wood on both sides of the head until the line of the neck flows in a smooth slightly hollow curve from the body up and towards the top of the mane and the cheeks.

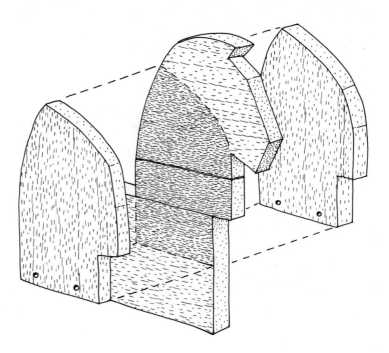

Fig. 14-5. The head and body. Cut, fit, and glue the head to the neck and the neck to the body. Clamp up and screw the slab sides to the head.

When you are carving, don't try for realism, just settle for a beautiful smooth-sweeping stylized form. When you have a good shape, work the surface of the wood so that all the faces, edges, and contours look to run with smooth curves, into each other. Resharpen the gouge and systematically shape the whole head to leave the surface of the wood looking pleasantly rippled and textured.

Finally, take the graded sandpapers and, being careful not to dull the crisp tooling, work over the form and bring it to good order.

CUTTING AND FIXING THE LEGS AND BARREL DISCS

Take the two body discs, which should measure about 5 inches in diameter, and tidy them up to a crisp edge and a smooth face. Take the four legs and work them with a rasp and sandpaper until the sawn faces are smooth and all the edges and corners are slightly rounded. Set the six pieces of wood— the two discs and the four legs—out on the workbench and pair them up so there are two legs to each disc.

With a compass, pencil, square, measure, and ruler, mark the two discs so that each has a 1-inch-wide central margin that goes from top to bottom, and a "top-of-leg" line that crosses the margin at right angles at a point about 1½ inches from the top. Now, a disc at a time, take a length of 1-inch-wide scrap and fit and fix a temporary guide strip up through the 1-inch-wide

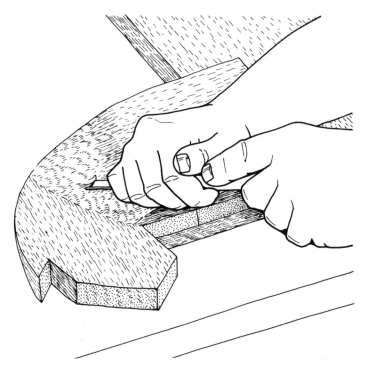

Fig. 14-6. *Carving the head. Use a gouge to cut away the waste at the top end of the neck.*

central margin; these guides need to be removed once the legs are fitted, so only hold them with a couple of tacks.

Place the discs, guide-strip up, on the bench and position the legs so that the top ends are butted hard up against both the guide strip and the "top-of-leg" mark. When you are sure that the legs are correctly positioned as described, fix with glue and screws (FIG. 14-7).

FITTING THE BODY PLANK
AND BUILDING THE BARREL

Start with a trial fitting, that is remove the temporary guide strips from the body discs and slide the ends of the body plank into position between the pairs of legs. If necessary, ease and shape the ends of the plank and the leading edge of the horse's head to make a good fit. Smear glue on the plank ends, wedge and adjust the fitting so that the structure stands firm and four-square, and then drive the screws home.

Take two of the 1-inch-wide, ½-inch-thick body strips, and place them side by side so that they run squarely from the tail to the point where the back of the head springs out from the body plank (FIG. 14-8). Have a close up look at the way the ends of the strips meet the body discs; see how, for a perfect fit, the sides of the strips need to be slightly undercut, then take the rasp or plane and remove the waste accordingly. Of course as you are fitting square-sided sections around a circular profile there will be small open spaces between the underside of the strips and the edge of the discs, but this is acceptable and within the character of the project.

When you come to fixing the strips between front and back legs, glue and pin scraps to the inside leg areas and use these as fixing points. And so you continue, shaping, fitting, adjusting, gluing, and nailing the 20 or so strips until you have built what you consider is good solid barrel like form.

Finally, tap the nail heads well below the surface of the wood, take off the sharp corners with the rasp, and fill the holes and blemishes with the auto body filler.

BUILDING THE BASE AND PUTTING TOGETHER

Take the two cut-to-size base boards and place them side by side and face down on the worksurface. Take the rasp and work the two mating edges until they are a good fit. Ideally you should be able to hold the boards up and not be able to see light between the mating edges. Take two battens and, with the boards still face down, set them squarely across the two boards at a point about 5 inches from the ends.

Chamfer the strip ends, have another check for board-to-strip squareness and then fit and fix with glue and screws. When you have achieved a base board that measures about 10 to 12 inches wide and about 14 to 15 inches long, set it better face down on the workbench. Take the four axle blocks, make sure that the ¾-inch-diameter axle holes are clean cut, and then glue

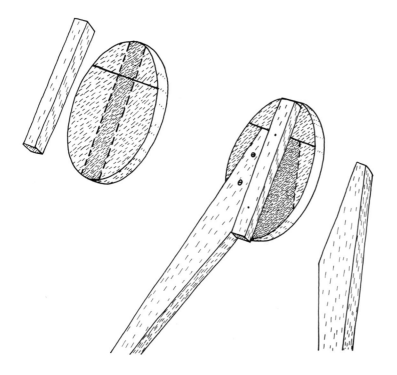

Fig. 14-7. Fixing the legs and barrel discs. (left to right) Butt the top of the legs hard up to the guide strip and to the "top of leg" marks.

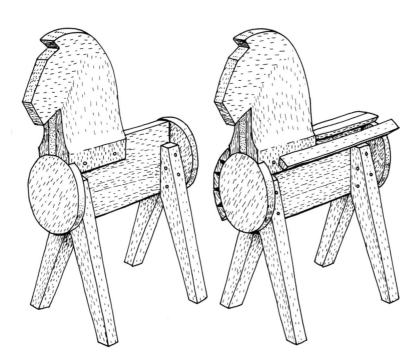

Fig. 14-8. Building the barrel. Slide the body plank into position between the pairs of legs. Place the slightly undercut body strips side-by-side around the discs.

and screw them in place. If all is as described, the blocks should be fitted so that the axles occur about 2 inches from the ends of the base.

Turn the board over so that it is best face up, set the horse fair and square on the board then take a pencil and mark in the position of the four leg holes. Now, with mallet and chisel, carefully chop out the four leg recesses (or blind mortises) to a depth of about ½ inch (FIG. 14-9). Work each hole in two stages; first chop out the four sides and establish the depth, then chamfer and cut back one side so that the angled leg drops in to a good firm fit.

When you have adjusted the fitting so that the four hooves butt securely and squarely in the four holes, fix with glue and screws. Finally, take the two axles, cut the end slots, slide them through the axle blocks, and fit and fix the wheels with glue and wedges.

PAINTING AND FITTING OUT

Because this horse might be used by a tender skinned toddler, take a knife, filler, and the graded sandpapers and make absolutely sure that the whole project is free from exposed screw and nail heads, sharp edges, splinters and rough corners. Clean up the dust and debris, wipe the horse over with a turpentine dampened cloth and move to the painting area.

Apply at least two generous coats of white primer and then—making sure that you allow the paint to dry out between coats and that you rub down dribbles and blobs—lay on two undercoats and the top gloss coat.

While you are waiting for the paint to dry look at the various painting ideas and see how it is possible to achieve any number of exciting designs (FIG. 14-2). For example you could go for a square patchwork pattern and scalloped reins to make a knight in armor charger. Or if you like the idea of a dappled horse you could paint and stencil round circles of masking tape. However, see how we have gone for a simple black stippling on a white background.

When the coat of white gloss enamel is completely dry, take a scrap of rag or sponge, a fine-point brush, and your chosen colors and paint all the details that go to make up the design. Stipple and dab-in the black speckled coat texture, line-in the eyes and the mane. Paint the base and the wheels good strong primary colors, such as blue for the base and red for the wheels (FIG. 14-10).

When the paint is dry lay on a generous coat of high gloss yacht varnish. Bore a ¾-inch-diameter hole through the rear disc and glue and pin the hank of tail yarn into position. Finally, take the narrow leather straps, a hammer, and the dome-headed upholstery tacks and fit the harness and bridle.

HINTS

You might build up the body and the legs with thicker pieces of easy-to-cut wood, like lime, and carve a more realistic and shapely form.

You could fit "hair" on both the mane and the tail.

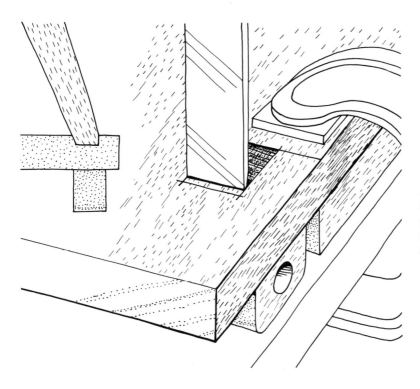

Fig. 14-9. Putting together. Chop out the four leg recesses to a depth of ½ inch. See how the base is supported with off-cuts.

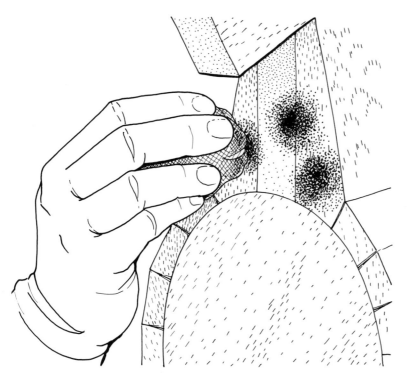

Fig. 14-10. Fitting out. Stipple and dab-in the black texture. It is wise to wear rubber gloves.

If you are worried about the horse being banged into furniture, or if you think a child may hurt himself on a sharp edge of the horse, you could attach padded bumpers.

Use a two-tube resin filler for car bodies rather than plaster.

If you are trying to make a super-strong toy, use dome head coach bolts rather than screws.

If you really want to make a special toy you could use red leather, brass upholstery tack, brass rings, and such to give the horse a saddle, horse brasses, and stirrups.

Make sure that all your materials are nontoxic.

Making a
Bilboquet

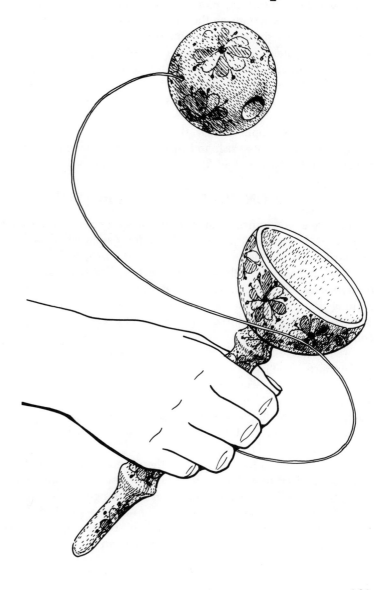

Fig. 15-1. A beautiful
traditional toy. The object is
to swing the ball up into the
air and then to catch it in the
cup.

THE GAME OF *BILBOQUET*, MORE COMMONLY KNOWN AS *CUP AND BALL*, IS a traditional game like skipping, diablo, or playing with a yo-yo, which is so ancient and universal that no one really knows when and where it was first played. All we know for sure is that prints and paintings suggest that it was very popular in sixteenth and seventeenth century France. Captain Cook in the eighteenth century reported that he saw the game being played by south sea islanders and by the Indians on the Northwest Coast of North America. In the late nineteenth and early twentieth century it was played in Japan, China, Mexico, Hawaii, and South America. The game probably developed independently and at the same time in many different countries. No doubt it was inspired by other ball-catching games, with the bilboquet cone a logical extension of a pair of cupped hands! From country to country there are many variations on the bilboquet theme, played with everything from paper cones, stuffed balls, pointed sticks, and feather shuttle cocks, to wicker work cones and leather covered balls.

The traditional game, as played in England, Europe, and America for the last 200 years, consists of a small wooden ball that is linked by a cord to a wooden handle, a handle that has a cone or cup on one end and a spike on the other.

The game is simple enough, the captive ball is flicked up into the air to the full extent of its leash and then it is either caught in the cup or on the spike (FIG. 15-1 and 15-3).

CONSIDERING THE PROJECT

If you have a wood-turning lathe with a special chuck (either a cup-chuck or a patent-chuck), and if you have a liking for making small, precisely turned and beautifully finished items, then this is the project for you.

Look at the working drawings and section details and see how although the actual form of a toy is relatively uncomplicated and straightforward with no hinged or pivotal parts, it is necessary to make a nicely fitting ball and cup; the materials and the various turning stages do require careful consideration.

For a small turning of this size and character, you need to use a strong fine-grained wood like boxwood, kingwood, rosewood, plum, cherry, holly, or yew. Contact a specialist supplier and see if they have some small "exotic" scraps. Also, you do need to use one or two special tools and pieces of equipment—a small spindle gouge, a sawtooth bit, and a cup-chuck. Before you consider starting out on this project, study the various illustrations and the tools and material list.

As to the actual form of the toy, there's no getting away from the fact that you do need to make a ball. When you make the handle, then there's room for considerable experimentation and design modification.

Of course the handle does need a cup on one end and a spike on the other, but that's not to say that the cup can't be shaped like a cone, an egg cup or a wine goblet. If you've always had a yen to test your skills by turn-

Fig. 15-2. *Painting grid.*

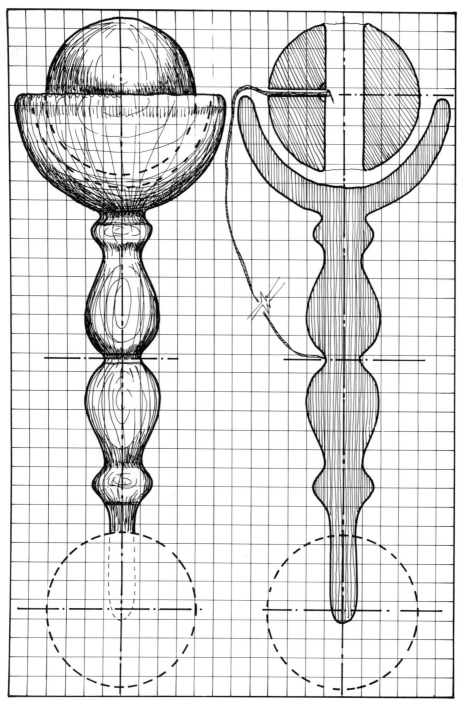

Fig. 15-3. Working drawings. At a scale of four grid squares to 1 inch, the ball is 2 inches in diameter and the cup measures about 7 inches long from the bottom of the handle to the rim.

ing off a fancy, curvy, many beaded show-piece, then now's your chance when you make the handle.

When I was a child I used to play with a modern cup and ball; the cup was spring loaded. Maybe you could modify the project and incorporate some sort of spring and trigger mechanism in the handle! Visit a museum collection and see as many ball and cup toys as possible. When you have seen eighteenth and nineteenth century European and American *bilboquets* and perhaps also those modern ones that are now being made in various ethnic communities around the world, and when you have examined our inspirational designs, sit down with a pencil, measure, and workout paper and draw your chosen form up to size (FIG. 15-2).

TOOLS AND MATERIALS

You need ✦ A piece of easy-to-turn close-grained wood at 3½ inches × 3½ inches square and about 14 inches long, you might use boxwood, cherry, plum, yew, or lignum vitae ✦ Workout paper ✦ Tracing paper ✦ Template cardboard ✦ Scissors ✦ A measure ✦ Pencils ✦ Calipers ✦ A rasp or plane ✦ The use of a lathe ✦ A cup- or patent-lathe chuck ✦ A tailstock drill chuck ✦ A good selection of wood-turning tools, these to include a small spindle gouge, a round-nosed scraper, and a parting tool ✦ A vise ✦ Graded sandpapers ✦ A hand drill with three drill bits at ⅛ inch, ¼ inch, and ½ inch diameter ✦ A small saw ✦ About 24 inches of coat = hanger wire ✦ A pair of pliers ✦ Wood primer ✦ Undercoat ✦ Acrylic paints, colors to suit ✦ A selection of medium- and fine-point brushes ✦ A tin of yacht varnish ✦ 24 inches of fine twine, best if braided ✦ Finally, you will need newspapers, cloths, and paint tubs

DESIGNING AND PREPARING THE WOOD FOR THE LATHE

When you have drawn your designs up to size and made sure that you have established good clean workable profiles, make careful tracings and pencil-press transfer the various profiles through to your pieces of template card. Line in the three templates—the ball, the cup, and the handle profiles—and cut them out. Take the 14-inch length of wood and check it over just to make sure that it is free from splits, dead knots, and stains.

Draw diagonals across the square-cut ends of the wood and with the compass set at a radius of 1½ inches, inscribe the ends with 3-inch-diameter circles. Mark off pencil tangents to the circles to make octagons and establish the areas of waste by drawing lines from the octagon corners down the length of the wood. Swiftly clear away the waste with a rasp, plane, or drawknife, until the wood is octagonal.

Punch in center marks at both ends of the wood. Position one end on the prong-center on the lathe, tap it in place, and then secure the work by clamping the tailstock in position and running the dead center tightly into the wood. Ease back the dead-center hand wheel just a fraction and oil the spin hole. Finally, position the tool rest so that it is as close as possible to the work and just below the center line.

ROUGHING OUT THE CYLINDER
AND MAKING THE BALL

When you are absolutely sure that the lathe is in good order, run through your pre-switch-on check list (see the Glossary), then turn it on. Take the round-nosed chisel and start by making a few practice runs up and down the work just to get the feel of your tool and the wood. For the first few cuts the tool will bump and judder, so take it easy until you have turned off the unevenness.

When you have turned the wood down to a cylinder, set the calipers at a gap of 3 inches and work toward a smooth face 3-inch-diameter cylinder. When you have achieved a good 3-inch-diameter cylinder, take a pencil and ruler, and at an inch or so in from the right-hand end of the wood, draw two lines that are 2⅛ inches apart. With the tools of your choice and the calipers set at 2 inches, turn away the waste on both sides of the two lines and then gradually turn the central 2⅛-inch section down to a 2-inch-diameter ball. You should reach a point where the ball looks to be pivoted between two small cones.

When you have turned the wood down to a slightly oversized sphere, check the form with the "half ball" template and then carefully trim the

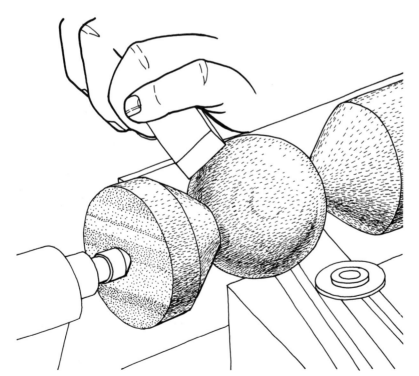

Fig. 15-4. Roughing out and making the ball. Clear away the end-of-ball waste and cut the surface of the ball down to a good smooth finish.

surface of the ball to a good finish (FIG. 15-4). When you have achieved what you consider is a good ball, take the graded sandpapers and rub the wood down to a good finish.

Finally, remove the work from the lathe and cut the ball off with the small straight saw.

MAKING THE CUP AND HANDLE

By the time you have turned off a 2-inch-diameter ball from your 14-inch-long cylinder—and allowing for the fact that one end of the wood now comes to a point—you should be left with a piece that is about 10 inches long. With the length of wood still mounted between centers, reduce the diameter of the pointed end until it fits your cup- or patent-chuck.

Mount the pointed end of the cylinder in the patent-chuck, make sure that the work is secure, then fit the flat-sawtooth bit into the drill chuck at the tailstock end of the lathe. Switch on the power, and with the tailstock locked into position, run the sawtooth bit into the end of the cylinder to a depth of about 1½ inches.

With the tools of your choice—you might use a gouge or a scraper or a combination of both—and remembering to make frequent checks with the "inside cup" template, bring the inside of the cup to a good size and finish (FIG. 15-5).

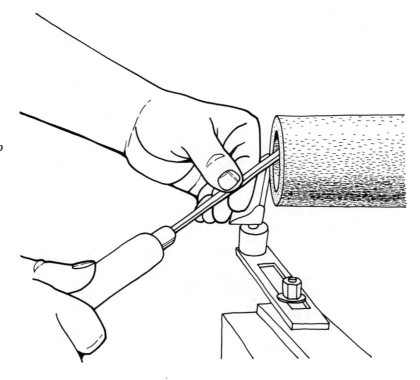

Fig. 15-5. Making the cup and handle. Hollow turn the cup interior and take it to a good finish.

Remove the sawtooth bit and take the cone shaped off-cut and trim it to shape so that it fits the mouth of the cup. Locate the cone plug in the cup and support it with a little gentle pressure from the tailstock (FIG. 15-6, top).

With pencil, measure, template, and parting tool, mark off the remaining length of wood with all the hollows and make a pilot cut at the center of each hollow to register depth. Turn off all the waste and work toward all the convex and concave curves and beads that make up the design (FIG. 15-6, bottom). Now—not forgetting to make frequent checks with the calipers on the wall thickness of the cup—take the graded sandpapers and rub the work down to a smooth finish.

Finally, take the work off the lathe, cut off the waste with the straight saw and rub the saw-cut pointed end of the handle down to good finish.

DRILLING, PAINTING, AND PUTTING TOGETHER

With the ball secured sawn-face up in the jaws of a muffled vise, take the ½-inch-diameter drill, and being careful not to apply too much pressure and split the grain, bore a hole right through the work (FIG. 15-7). Imagine that the ½-inch entrance and exit holes are the North and South Poles of the earth. Secure the ball so that the equator line is uppermost, and bore a ⅛-inch-diameter hole through the side of the ball and into the ½-inch bore. Take

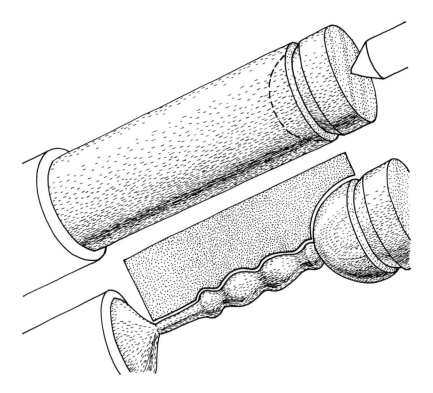

Fig. 15-6. Making the cup and handle. (top) Locate the cone plug in the cup and support it with the tailstock. (bottom) Turn the cylinder down to a good template fit.

the ¼-inch-diameter drill, and with the ball repositioned so that the ½-inch hole is once again uppermost, angle the drill down into the wood and countersink the exit point of the ⅛-inch hole.

With the handle secured in the jaws of the muffled vise, take the ⅛-inch-diameter drill and bore a single hole through the halfway point, or the "waist." Rub down the various holes, make sure that all surfaces and edges are smooth, clean off the dust, and move to the painting area.

Arrange your paints and brushes so that they are handy, and set the two turnings up, ready for painting, on wire and scrap wood stands (clip off two 6-inch lengths of coat-hanger wire, stick them into the bench or a piece of scrap wood and spike them into the ⅛-inch-diameter cord holes in the ball and the handle).

Lay on the primer, an undercoat, the top or ground coat, the various patterns and motifs that go to make up the design, and a generous coat of varnish, with adequate drying intervals. When the varnish is dry, take the cord and attach the ball to the cup; tie one end to the handle, then, and—this is a little more tricky—take the ball, thread the other end of the cord through the small ⅛-inch-diameter hole and out of the large spike hole (FIG. 15-8).

Finally, knot the end, draw the knot back into the countersunk hole, and the job is done!

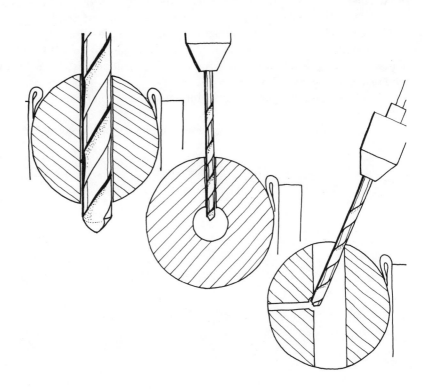

Fig. 15-7. Drilling, painting, and putting together. (left to right) Drill a ½-inch-diameter hole through the ball. Drill a ⅛-inch-diameter hole through the side of the ball and into the main hole. Use a ¼-inch drill bit to countersink the exit of the ⅛-inch hole.

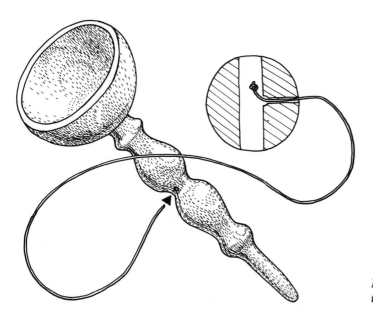

Fig. 15-8. Putting together. Tether the ball to the cup handle.

HINTS

If you don't have a cup-chuck or a patent-chuck, but you do have a small screw-chuck, then it's possible to make a deep glue-spigot chuck. A large blank of wood is fixed to a screw-chuck, which is bored out to take the spigot diameter. The workpiece is glued into the bore hole.

If you like the idea of a *bilboquet*, but don't want to go to the trouble of making a ball, then there's no reason why you can't attach a small ready-made rubber or plastic ball.

If you consider the handle spike a bit dangerous, then modify the design to leave it out.

When you choose the cord, go for a limp braided type like cotton or linen.

Making a
Trundle
Market Truck

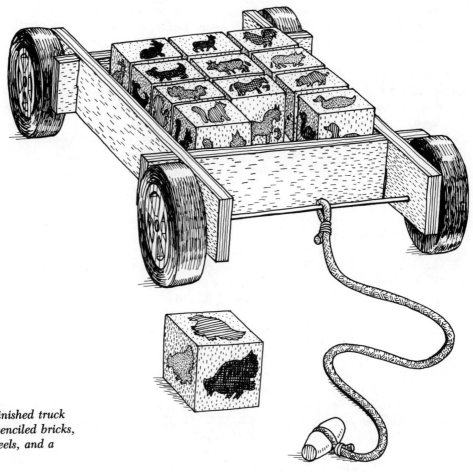

*Fig. 16-1. The finished truck
complete with stenciled bricks,
shop bought wheels, and a
pull-rope.*

CHILDREN LOVE TOYS WITH WHEELS! FOR INSTANCE: TRUNDLE TRUCKS; PULL-along vehicles with rope and toggle handles; baby walkers; farm wagons; cars; pull-along horses; market carts; trams; trollies; and trains. If a toy can be pushed, pulled or trundled along on wheels, then not only is it good fun, but the play and learning potential is enormous.

And picture blocks, beloved by children of just about every country and period, are also very good learning toys. The educational play concept of having blocks with numbers, pictures, and letters on the faces is so simple and yet so sophisticated that it really does take a bit of a beating. The blocks can be piled one on top of another. The faces can be arranged so that the letters spell out words or arranged so that the images come together to make pictures, and so on. There's only one thing better than a trundle truck and a pile of picture bricks, and that's an "off to market" pull truck!

CONSIDERING THE PROJECT

Have a look at the working drawings and the various pictures and designs, and see how this project is only a market truck in the sense that the stencil printed motifs on the block faces relate to domestic farmyard animals (FIGS. 16-1 through 16-3). If you like the idea of picture blocks in a wheeled box, but you don't much like the animal motifs, then there's no reason why you shouldn't change the designs to suit you. If you have a passion for cars, architecture, zoo animals, fruit, or the ABCs, all you have to do is to change the imagery accordingly.

See how, at a scale of one grid square to 1 inch, the truck measures 15 inches long, 9 inches wide, and 1½ inches deep, with the bricks being 2-inch cubes. The bricks are made from a length of 2- × -2-inch prepared beech, while the truck is made from ½-inch-thick multi-ply. Note the use of a set of ready-made wheels.

The construction is very basic; the sides are lap-slotted at the corners and the base is glued and screwed directly onto the boxed sides. As for the motifs, the plain wood surfaces are varnished, and the designs are stencil printed using plastic contact film and quick-dry acrylics.

Have a good look at the designs, visit museums and toy shops, consider making modifications, and then sit down with a pencil, measure, and workpad and draw the designs out to size (FIG. 16-2).

TOOLS AND MATERIALS

You need ✦ An 18- × -18-inch square sheet of ½-inch-thick multi-ply ✦ A 30-inch length of prepared beech at 2- × -2-inches square ✦ Workout paper ✦ Tracing paper ✦ Pencil and ruler ✦ A set square ✦ A straight saw ✦ A coping saw ✦ The use of workbench with a vise ✦ A pack of graded sandpapers ✦ A rasp ✦ A ½-wide file ✦ Four 3-inch-diameter plastic wheels, color and type to suit ✦ Two mild-steel axle rods 9 inches long, to fit the wheels (the axles must have patent end fixings) ✦ A hand drill, with a drill bit to suit the size of the axles ✦ PVA glue ✦ Twenty

Fig. 16-2. Painting or stenciling grid.

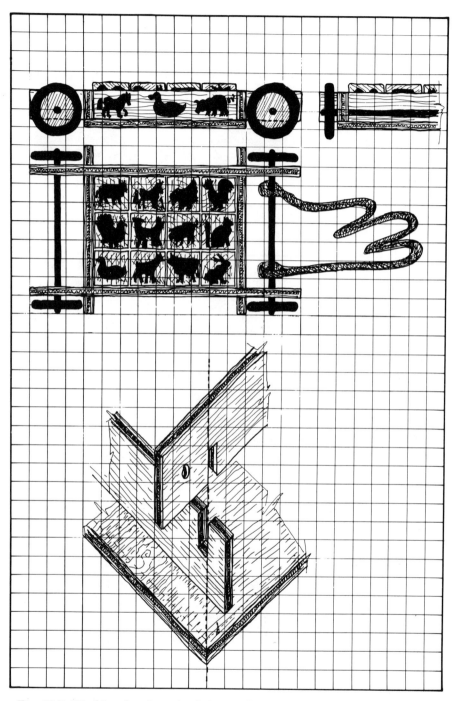

Fig. 16-3. Working drawings. (top) At a scale of one grid square to 1 inch, the truck measures 15 inches long and 9 inches wide. Note the simple joints and the use of shop bought wheels.

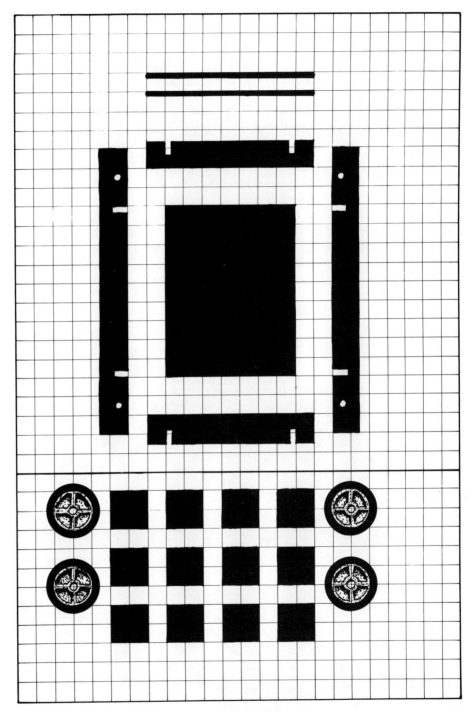

Fig. 16-4. Cutting grid.

1-inch-long brass screws ✦ A screwdriver ✦ A tin of yacht varnish ✦ A brush for the varnish ✦ A sheet of clear-plastic contact film, as used by air-brush artists and graphic designers ✦ A fine-point scalpel ✦ A cutting board ✦ A pair of scissors ✦ Acrylic paints, best to use primary colors ✦ A stencil brush ✦ And odds and ends like newspaper, masking tape, and cloths

SETTING OUT THE DESIGNS AND CUTTING THE WOOD

Study the various working drawings and details for a clear understanding of how the project is fabricated. Finalize all your working drawing details and transfer the lines of the design through to your wood. The five pieces that make up the truck are set out on the ½-inch-thick ply, and the piece of 2- × 2-inch-square beech is stepped off along its length at 2¹⁄₁₆-inch intervals. Bear in mind that the old toymaker's adage is "measure twice and cut once," so make sure that the measurements are accurate.

Use the straight saw to cut out the five plywood parts (FIG. 16-5). Use the rasp and the sandpapers to prepare a good, smooth, crisp-edged, and finished wood surface.

A piece at a time, take the four 1½-inch-wide strips, secure them in the jaws of the vise, and use the coping saw and the ½-inch-wide file to achieve the eight ½-inch-wide, 1½-inch-long lap slots.

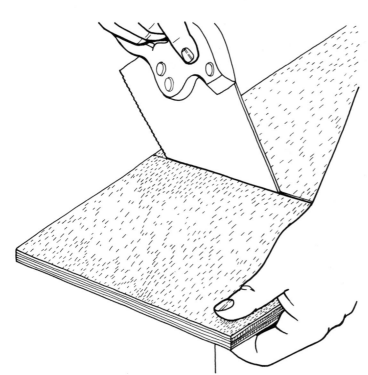

Fig. 16-5. Setting out. Use a straight saw to cut the ½-inch-thick plywood sides and base. When you come to the end of a cut, support the board with your hand to avoid splitting the wood.

PUTTING THE TRUCK TOGETHER
AND FITTING THE WHEELS

When the eight slots have been cut and all five pieces of plywood are a good fit and finish, take the four side pieces, glue the slots, and fit them together. Now dribble a little PVA glue around the bottom edge of the sides, drill pilot holes, and then screw the base to the sides (FIG. 16-6).

When you come to fitting the 3-inch-diameter wheels, take note of the base-to-side height of 2 inches, and mark out the four axle holes so that they occur 1 inch down from the top edge of the truck and 1½ inches in from the end. Drill the four axle holes with a bit that matches the axles's diameter. Slide the axles home, locate the wheels, and attach the patent hub-to-axle caps/pins. Tidy up rough areas with a scrap of sandpaper and lay on a coat of varnish.

CUTTING AND DECORATING THE BLOCKS

Take the straight saw and the length of 2-×2-inch-square beech and, allowing for the thicknesses of the saw kerf, cut the wood into 2-inch lengths (FIG. 16-7). Block at a time, use the rasp, file, and the graded sandpaper, to rub the wood to a good smooth 2-inch cube finish. Give them a coat of clear varnish and put them to one side to dry out.

While the varnish is drying, look at the various animal motifs. Note the basic, uncomplicated, easy-to-cut profiles. Cut the plastic film into 12 squares

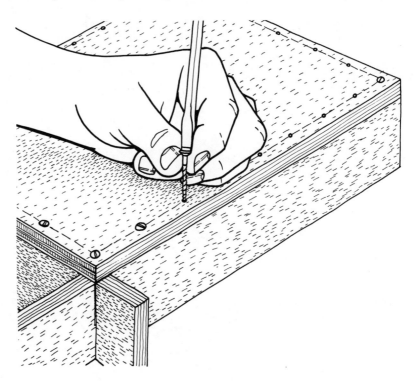

Fig. 16-6. Putting together. Glue and screw-fix the base to the sides.

at 2 × 2 inches. Now, a square at a time, position the film, paper-side up, over the motifs and trace off the lines of the design.

With the traced lines clearly established, and the film secured, plastic-side up, on the workboard, take the fine-point scalpel and cut out the design "windows." Work with a careful controlled action, all the while drawing the point of the scalpel toward you and maneuvering the work so that the scalpel blade is always presented with the line of next cut.

PRINTING THE STENCILS

Select one of the blocks, wipe it over with a dry cloth, and set it faceup, on the worksurface. Take one of the stencil plates, peel away the backing paper, and arrange the plate on the block so that the motif appears to be standing square.

When you are happy with the arrangement, press and smooth the plastic with a soft cloth to remove all wrinkles and air bubbles. Continue until all the blocks have been paired off with a stencil plate.

When you print the designs, take a small amount of stiffish paint up on the stencil brush and carefully block in the stencil plate window with a delicate up-and-down pecking action (FIG. 16-8).

Work the motif from side-to-center. Make sure that you don't force paint under the edge of the plastic film. When one or more faces of all the blocks have been printed, peel off the plastic stencil plates, wait awhile for the paint

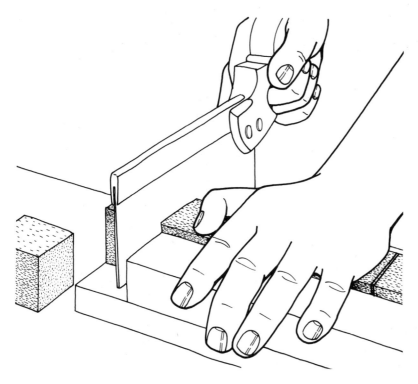

Fig. 16-7. Cutting the blocks. Using a straight saw and a bench hook, cut the 2-inch × 2-inch wood down into lengths that are a fraction over 2 inches. The little extra allows for sawing and sanding wastage.

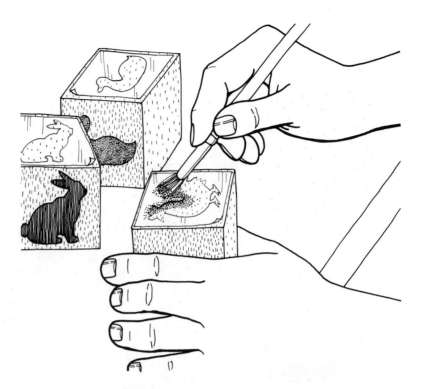

Fig. 16-8. Printing the stencils. Block-in the stencil windows with an up-and-down side-to-center brushing action.

to dry, and lay on another coat of varnish. Finally, knot both ends of a length of soft, fat, braided cotton rope to one axle, and the job is done.

HINTS

The rope makes this a "pull" truck. If you want to make a "push-and-pull" truck, attach a wooden handle with a broomstick crossbar.

If you want to make more of the rope, it could be fitted with either a metal ring or a couple of wooden toggles.

You could extend the stencil printing part of the project and run the design around the sides of the truck.

Children like boxes with lids. You could modify the project, and fit either a sliding or hinged lid.

Making a
Wibble-Wobble
Tumble Doll

Fig. 17-1. The weighted
base ensures that the doll
always wobbles upright.

KNOWN IN ENGLAND AS *WIBBLE-WOBBLES* OR *TUMBLERS*, IN AMERICA AS *Kellys*, in Germany as *Putzelmann*, in France as *poupee boule*, in Japan as *Ot-tok-l*, in China as *pan-puh-too*, and variously around the world as *tilters, stand-up dolls, knock-down Dutch dolls, Deutsch tumblers* and even *Fanny Royd's*, the little tumble doll figure with its half-ball base must surely be one of the simplest and yet funniest toys of all time.

Traditionally made from turned and carved wood, but now more often than not made of plastic or paper-mache, these little toys are great fun. Give them a push and they wobble over, do an odd jerky dance, and then bob back up again.

It's easy to see why children still enjoy playing with tumble dolls; who could not find pleasure in their funny antics and colorful imagery? But more than that, I think children are fascinated by this toy because the workings are something of a mystery. There are no obvious strings, pulleys, or levers, and no clockwork or elastic motors to be wound up.

So how does the tumble doll manage to maintain his happy-go-lucky equilibrium? Like all traditional toys, the answer is beautifully simple. The tumble doll has a low center of gravity and a lead-weight concealed in its half-ball base. From the toymaker's point of view the tumbler is a delightful, relatively easy-to-make ingenious moving toy.

If you have a lathe, a liking for small enigmatic playthings, and you are looking to make a traditional toy for the playroom or even your office desk, then without doubt this is the project for you.

CONSIDERING THE PROJECT

First of all, have a look at the project picture and see how we have veered away from the tradition of having male tumblers like clowns, boys, gods, sages, and old men. We have gone for a buxom lady, one dressed in a traditional European peasant-type costume (FIG. 17-1). Look at the working drawings and see how at a grid scale of four squares to 1 inch—that is one square to ¼ inch—our well-rounded tumbler lady measures about 3 inches wide and 4 inches high (FIGS. 17-2 and 17-3.)

Study the cross-section and see how we have achieved the lead-weighted base simply by hollowing out the bottom of the turning, filling the cavity with a mixture of lead shot and resin, and then replugging the hole prior to finishing. Even though this toy has an uncomplicated form it must be precisely turned and well finished.

Before you finalize your working drawings and start fixing sizes and such, take a trip to the nearest toy museum and or ethnic craft shop and see if you can come up with a modification that is an improvement upon our design; perhaps a more exciting form or maybe a simpler weight mechanism.

Note: Because this is primarily a toddler toy, one that might be sucked, chewed, dropped, and generally bounced around the playroom, we have avoided fragile and complicated additions like pivotal arms and bells. Keep this in mind if you do decide to make modifications.

Fig. 17-2. Painting grid. It is possible to achieve all manner of doll characters.

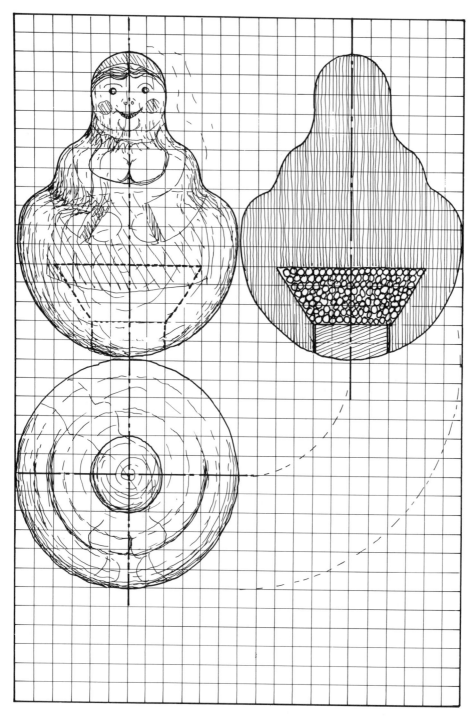

Fig. 17-3. Working drawings. At a scale of four grid squares to 1 inch the doll
is 4 inches high and 3 inches wide. Note the weighted base and the plug.

TOOLS AND MATERIALS

You need ✦ A piece of close grained wood at about 3¼ inches × 3 ¼ inches square and 5 inches long, you might use soft maple, cherry, sycamore, or apple ✦ Workout paper ✦ Tracing paper ✦ A pencil and measure ✦ A rasp, plane, or drawknife ✦ A pair of calipers ✦ A tailstock drill chuck ✦ A 1-inch-diameter flat or sawtooth drill bit ✦ The use of a small lathe ✦ A small faceplate ✦ Screws to fit the faceplate ✦ A screwdriver ✦ A special multi-chuck with a 1-inch-diameter expanding pin ✦ A selection of wood-turning tools ✦ A pack of graded sandpapers ✦ A quantity of lead shot ✦ A small amount of resin glue ✦ A 1-inch-diameter plug cutter ✦ A small hammer ✦ A selection of broad—and fine-point brushes ✦ Varnish ✦ Model maker's enamel paints, colors to suit ✦ And finally you need all the usual workshop bits and pieces like a pair of compasses, rags, turpentine, newspapers, and paint tubs

STARTING OUT

Check your piece of wood to make sure that it is free from flaws. Draw diagonals across the square ends, punch in center points, and inscribe 3-inch-diameter circles. Draw tangents to the circles to create octagons. Once you have established the areas of waste, use the plane, rasp, or drawknife to cut the wood down to a rough octagonal section.

This done, screw the faceplate to one end of the wood, mount it on the mandrel or left-hand drive center, and wind up the tailstock so that the wood is secure. Make sure that the lathe is in good order, see to it that your hair and clothes are safely tied back, position the tool rest, and switch on.

Present the chisel to the work, make a few passes just to get the feel of the tool and the wood, and then set about clearing away the rough. Finally, turn the wood down to a 3-inch-diameter cylinder.

TURNING THE HALF-BALL,
HOLLOWING OUT AND TURNING THE PROFILE

When you have turned a smooth cylinder, use the tools of your choice to round off the shoulders at the right-hand end of the work (FIG. 17-4). Don't try at this stage to achieve anything like a perfectly finished half-ball, just settle for clearing away the rough and establishing the overall profile.

When you have removed most of the waste, wind the tailstock back so that it is well clear of the work, and reposition the T-rest so that it is set over the center of the lathe bed and as near as possible to the partially turned half-ball. Complete the turning by taking the half-ball to a perfect smooth finish; if necessary, check the profile by making and using a half-circle template.

When you have what you consider is a good half-ball form, switch off the lathe and mount the 1-inch-diameter sawtooth drill in a drill chuck at the tailstock. Switch on and carefully wind up the tailstock to drive the drill bit into the end of the half-ball; aim to cut a hole that is about 1¼ inches deep (FIG. 17-4).

Now take the small spindle gouge, or perhaps a hooked scraper, and being careful not to damage the mouth of the hole, hollow out the inside of the lower-half base. Note: If you do decide to use a hooked scraper, switch off the lathe before you draw the tool out of the hole.

Now take the work off the lathe and remove the faceplate. Screw the multi-chuck on the mandrel. Slide the work on the chuck and open up the 1-inch-diameter pin until the work is a tight secure fit. With the tool rest placed variously at the side and front-center, turn off the outside of the figure.

Finally, when you have achieved the smooth-curved form, use the graded sandpapers to take the wood to a perfect finish (FIG. 17-5).

WEIGHTING AND PLUGGING

Arrange the figure in a box or can so that the hole is uppermost, and set out the lead shot and the resin glue. First find out how much shot you need by filling up the hollow to about ⅝ inch of the rim. Empty the shot out of the figure and into a little tub or dish. Add the hardener to the resin glue. Stir in the shot.

Then being careful not to get it on the outside of the turning—you might use a paper funnel—pour the whole sticky mixture into the base of the figure to within ½ inch of the rim (FIG. 17-6).

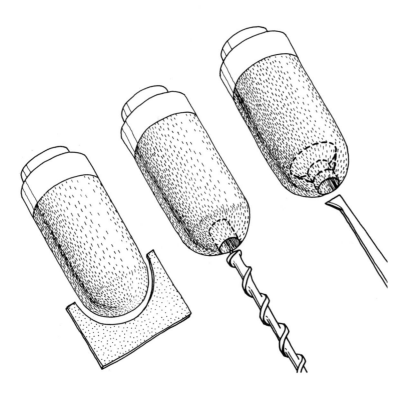

Fig. 17-4. Turning and hollowing out. (left to right) Cut the end of the cylinder down to a half-ball and check the form with the template. Bore out a 1-inch-diameter, 1¼-inch-deep base hole. Hollow-turn the inside lower half of the base.

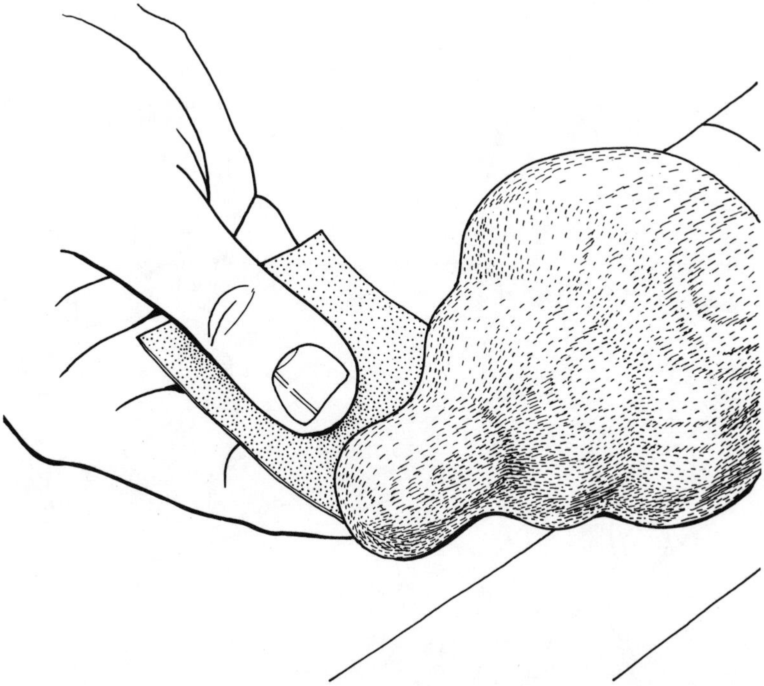

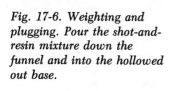

Fig. 17-5. Turning the profile. When you have achieved the doll form, use the graded sandpapers to rub the wood down to a good finish.

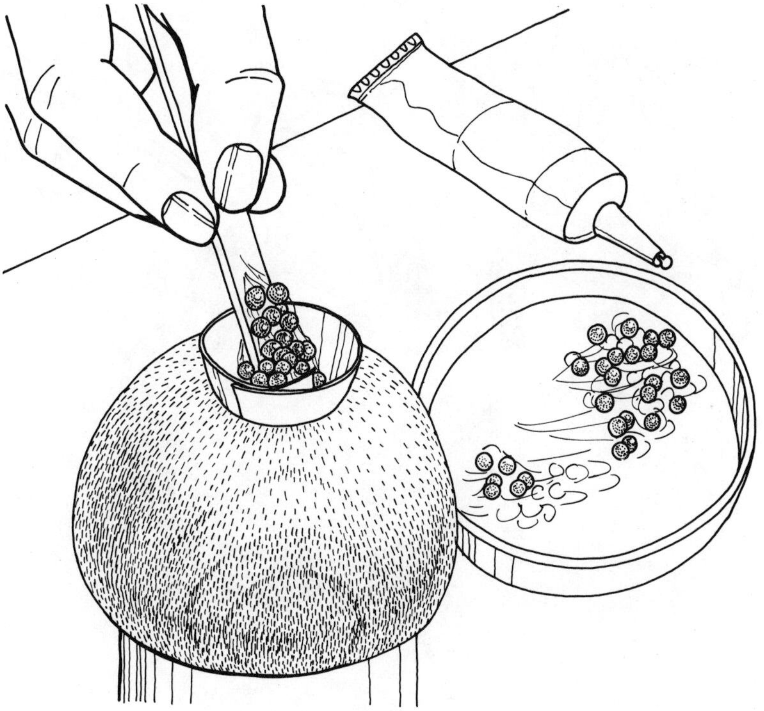

Fig. 17-6. Weighting and plugging. Pour the shot-and-resin mixture down the funnel and into the hollowed out base.

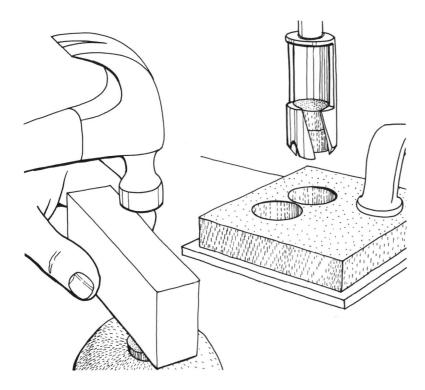

Fig. 17-7. Weighting and plugging. Cut a 1-inch-diameter plug. Apply a little glue to the plug and tap it into the hole to leave it slightly proud.

Fig. 17-8. Painting. (left) Support the work on three pins and set it up in the painting area. (right) Lay on the main blocks of color and pick out the details.

Now, cut a 1-inch diameter, ½-inch-thick plug and tap it into the hole so that it protrudes slightly (FIG. 17-7). Finally, take the graded sandpapers and rub the plug down until it is smooth and flush with the rest of the turned half-ball.

FINISHING AND PAINTING

Prior to painting, tap three long ball-head pins into the base of the figure and set it up in the painting area. Start by laying on a coat of varnish. When the varnish is dry—and not forgetting to let the paints dry out between coats—lay on the main blocks of color. Paint the details with a fine brush, lay on another coat of varnish, and the job is done (FIG. 17-8).

HINTS

If you like the idea of making a tumble doll but consider the techniques too complicated or whatever, you could simplify the form and go for a round-ended cylinder.

If you don't have a multi-chuck with a 1-inch-diameter pin, you can modify the project and turn off your own wooden spigot chuck.

When you are turning out the hollow, be careful that you don't make the sides of the half-ball too thin. Aim for a base that is no thinner than ⅜ inch.

If you can't get hold of any shot, you could use a piece of salvaged lead and cast your own plug. Or you could pack the cavity with coins. Either way, test for weight before you drive the plug home.

Making a Thuringian
Milkmaid Doll

Fig. 18-1. When the cord is pulled, the little milkmaid figure looks to be plunging the churn pole up and down.

I N THURINGIA, A REGION IN SOUTHWEST EAST GERMANY, THERE IS A TRADITION of making curious woodcarved, string-operated moving manikins: little men that nod their heads and raise and lower their hats; peasant girls that lift babies high in the air; beautifully carved acrobats that lift their legs; cats and mice that play a never ending peekaboo game; little men that open and close their mouths, and so on.

From village to village, there has evolved a unique tradition of making all manner of wood carved and painted working toy figures that, at the pull of a string, perform one or more funny movements. Of course such toys are popular because the stiff, jerky, repetitious movements are in themselves comical. Who could not smile and find pleasure in a rosy apple-faced doll whose whole life is spent doffing his hat and bowing.

But more than that, I think such toys are especially fascinating because the workings are hidden and not easily understood. If you want to make a small, delicate, intricately mechanical toy, then this is the project for you (FIG. 18-1).

CONSIDERING THE PROJECT

Have a look at the working drawings and see how we have modified the design with plywood (FIG. 18-3). This is not to say that our toy is in any way less exciting than the genuine article, only that the fabrication techniques relate to sawing, cutting, and laminating rather than to turning and woodcarving.

See how—at a grid scale of four squares to 1 inch—the little milkmaid or butter-churning peasant girl stands about 5 inches high. Study the details and sections, and consider how the hollow figure is built up box-like from a number of plywood thicknesses.

Note especially the pivotal attachment of the arms to the body and the body to the hips, and the way the slot-pivot sliding fit of the hands to the buttechurn pole or staff allows for an easy, if slightly jerking, up-and-down movement. Most important of all, see that the bottom of the staff is lead-weighted, so the "at rest" position of the figure is with the back bent.

In use, as the string is pulled, the upper half of the body swings upright on its pivot; the arms appear to be lifting the butter-churn staff. And of course when the string is released, the lead weight pulls down on the staff, which in turn pulls down on the arms, which in turns pulls down on the upper half of the body—beautifully simple and direct, uniquely charming toy.

When you have studied all the sections and details, and when you have a clear understanding of how the toy is put together and why it works, then visit toy museums and craft shops, and see if you can search out other moving dolls that relate to the German toy making tradition (FIG. 18-3). Make sketches and notes, and draw out the various profiles to size (FIG. 18-4).

TOOLS AND MATERIALS

You need ✦ A sheet of best quality ¼-inch-thick multilayer plywood at about 12 × 12 inches—this allows for an easy fit and some waste ✦ Work-

Fig. 18-2. Painting grid.

Fig. 18-3. Working drawing. (top) At a grid scale of four squares to 1 inch, the figure stands about 5 inches high. Note the still-to-standing sequence of movement.

Fig. 18-4. Cutting grid. There are 24 cut-outs in all. If you have any doubts as to how the toy works, make a card-and-glue prototype.

out paper ✦ Tracing paper ✦ Masking tape ✦ Pencil and ruler ✦ A coping or fret saw ✦ A pack of spare saw blades ✦ A V-board, sometimes called a bird's-mouth fretwork board or even just a sawing vee ✦ A G-clamp ✦ About 6 inches of ⅛-inch-diameter hardwood doweling ✦ A length of fat, strong, smooth cord ✦ A hand drill with two drill bits, one at ⅛ inch and the other at 3/16 inch ✦ A large bead or button ✦ A pipe cleaner ✦ A pack of graded sandpapers ✦ A quantity of PVA glue ✦ A sharp clasp knife or scalpel ✦ A selection of paint brushes ✦ Undercoat ✦ A selection of acrylic paints ✦ Two lead washers at a ¼ inch thickness

FRETTING OUT THE PROFILES

When you have a clear picture in your mind's eye of how you want your figure to be, and when you have drawn up the 24 profiles to size (two arms, a single head and torso, two torso sides, a churn staff, two hand spacer washers, two skirt sides, six skirt spacers, two churn sides and lastly the six churn spacers) make sure all the lines are clean cut and well established, then make a good tracing (FIG. 18-4). You will also need a base piece at about 3½ × 3 inches.

Pencil-press transfer the traced lines through to the working face of the sheet of plywood. Clamp the Vee-board to the edge of the workbench and start fretting out all the profiles. With the wood positioned so that the line of cut is hanging just over the edge of the "V," take the coping saw and set to work.

Make sure that the blade passes through the plywood at right angles to the working face, and that the line of cut is slightly to the waste side of the drawn line. Carefully fret out the 24 shapes. Sand the pieces just to remove all the burrs and rough edges. Label the cut-outs, "arm right," "arm left," and so on, so you know which part is which, and where it fits in relationship to the whole.

LAMINATING, SANDING, AND DRILLING

When you have cut and clearly labeled all the parts that go to make up the total design, set them out in related stacks or groups. You will have eight parts that make up the skirt, three cut-outs that make the torso, eight churn pieces, and so forth (FIG. 18-5). When you are absolutely sure that all is correct, smear mating faces with PVA glue and clamp up. You should now have eight parts in all—the skirt, the torso, two arms, two hand washers, the churn staff, and the churn.

When the glue is dry, take the graded sandpapers and carefully sand all cut edges until they are smooth and well rounded. Establish the position of all holes—best check them off out against the working drawings—and bore them out.

Drill the shoulder and waist holes, (the holes through the torso) and the hand holes with the 3/16-inch-diameter bit; drill all other holes with a ⅛-inch

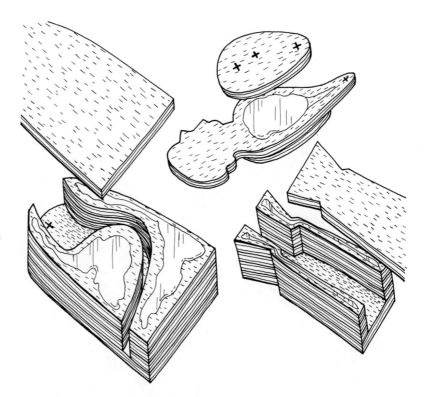

Fig. 18-5. Laminating, sanding, and drilling. Glue the eight parts that go to make up the skirt, the three parts for the torso, and the eight churn pieces.

bit. In broad terms the pivot rods need to be a tight fit in the skirt, arms, and staff, and a loose fit in the body and hands. Finally, take a fine-point knife and extend the hand holes along the wrists to make slots.

FITTING THE BODY PIVOTS AND STRING

When you have bored out the holes and you are sure that all is correct, take a scrap of sandpaper and sand the splinters and roughness. Now, clear away the clutter, and set out the skirt, the body, the two arms, the string, the knife, the glue, and the pipe cleaner.

First of all take the string and knot one end onto the body "tail"—make a firm secure knot. Pass the other end of the string through the pipe cleaner "needle" and carefully pass it down through the top of the skirt. Remember that the through-skirt passage is S curved and ease the flexible wire down through the hole until it comes out at the back of the skirt (FIG. 18-6).

Turn the body around so that it relates to the skirt and link them up with the dowel. Trim and fit the dowel so that it is a tight fixture in the skirt hole and a loose fit in the body.

With the torso fitting loosely on the waist pivot, glue the dowel in the skirt holes and trim the ends down to a good fit and finish.

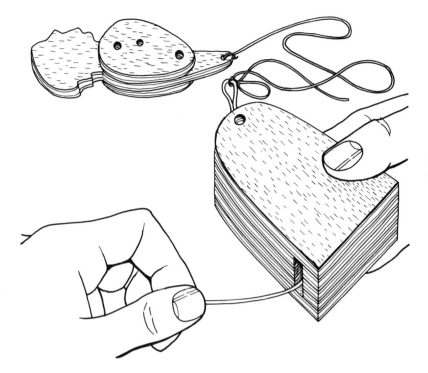

Fig. 18-6. Fitting the body pivots and the string. Ease the flexible "needle" down through the skirt hole.

FITTING THE ARMS, HANDS, AND CHURN

When the torso and skirt link-up has been achieved, then comes the difficult business of fitting the arms to the body, and the hands to the churn. First, push a short length of dowel through the "arm stop" hole (the hole through the middle of the torso) and trim it off so that a short dowel stub protrudes from each side of the body. Next, push one arm on the end of a length of dowel, pass the dowel through the body and dry push-fit the other arm.

Take a ¾-inch length of dowel and pass it through the "paddle" end of the churn pole. Put the lead washers on the dowel stubs and hold them in place with a dab of contact adhesive. Slide the long, thin end of the staff up through the bottom of the churn and push a 1½-inch length of dowel through the hand hole (the hole near the top end of the staff) to make the hand rod.

The next procedure is tricky, so be patient and take it slowly. With a scalpel or knife or even a scrap of sandpaper, carefully thin the last ¼ inch at each end of the hand rod, then put the little wooden washers and the hands on the rod and push the arms along the shoulder dowels toward the body, until the hands are a secure but loose fit (FIG. 18-7).

Now, place the figure and the churn on a flat surface—they need to be about ⅛ inch apart—and have a very delicate practice pull on the string. If all is well and as described, when the string is pulled the top half of the body will swing upright and the arms will rise up and appear to be lifting the churn plunger.

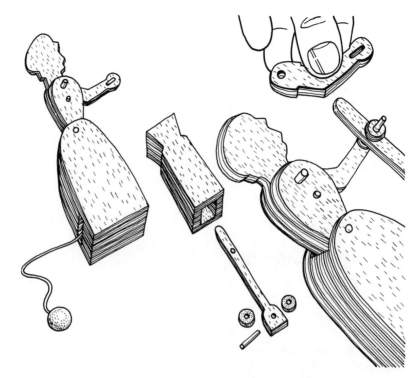

Fig. 18-7. Putting together. (left) Fix the lead washers to the bottom of the staff and pass it up through the base of the churn. (right) Locate the washers on the hand rods and the arms on the shoulder rods.

FITTING, FINISHING, AND PAINTING

When you have adjusted all the various holes, slots, and pivots so that the whole toy comes together to make a good fit, glue the figure and the churn on a base; then glue, fit, and trim all the dowels and pivots. Cut the string to length and attach a large bead or brass ring.

Sand the toy to a good smooth finish; make sure that all holes, dowel ends, edges, and corners are free from splinters and burrs.

Prepare the painting area. Apply a primer, an undercoat, the main ground colors, the decorative patterns and details, and a coat of varnish (FIG. 18-2) to finish the toy. Be sure to let the paints dry out between coats and remember that the paints are best applied in thin washes rather than heavy daubs.

HINTS

When you drill the various holes, it's vital that they be well placed. If you have any doubts, you can fix their position by making a card-and-clip prototype.

It is important that the string is an easy fit through the skirt tunnel. Use a plump string and make sure that all edges and corners are smooth and rounded. You might wax the tunnel.

The shape and size of the hand slot is best achieved by trial and error. Drill out a starter hole and modify its shape upon assembly. You could drill out two side-by-side holes and link them with a file or saw.

When painting close to the pivot points, make sure that the coats are thin and free from drips and runs.

Making a Set of Russian "Nest" Dolls

Fig. 19-1. The dolls' nest, one within another.

NEST TOYS ARE BEAUTIFUL! OPEN ONE LARGE BOX ONLY TO FIND ANOTHER inside, open this box to reveal yet another box, and so on. Most of us love the idea of small secret hand-size containers (FIG. 19-1). From country to country, there are many traditional nesting toys made from material such as wood and clay, woven fibers, nuts, and egg shells. The best of all, and certainly the most well know, are the nests of Russian dolls.

Turned, carved, and painted by peasants, these beautiful folk toys are usually worked in the form of plump old women or equally plump families; a diminishing series of figures all dressed in traditional costume.

Nests often contain 12 or more figures, with the largest being about 9 inches high and the smallest only as big as your little finger. These painted dolls are usually lathe turned and worked in the form of egg-shaped containers.

Take the top off the largest doll—a fat lady with a bright red scarf and a yellow smock—and there inside will be a slightly smaller lady with a yellow scarf and a red smock. As each doll is opened to reveal another doll inside, it can be seen that although the details of dress and pattern are more or less identical—with all the ladies wearing scarves, shawls, smocks and aprons—the main blocks of color are usually alternated to create exciting counterchange effects.

A variation on the fat lady theme is a figure painted in gold and silver with a long flowing head dress who is sometimes described as the Russian folk hero Yermak (FIG. 19-2).

If you are searching for a project to test your wood-turning skills, or if you want to create a traditional toy that might be enjoyed by young and old alike, then this is the project for you.

CONSIDERING THE PROJECT

Have a look at the gridded working drawings, and see how we have chosen to make a characteristic, smooth-profiled, plump lady nest of four dolls in the Russian folk tradition (FIG. 19-3). Note how—at a scale of four grid squares to 1 inch—the largest doll stands about 5 inches high while the smallest is a tiddler of just under 2 inches.

Study the working stages and see how, apart from the small solid doll, each doll is turned from one piece (both the base and the lid are turned from the same prepared cylinder of wood). We have chosen to use a wood-screw chuck and work through the fabrication stages in the order of cylinder blank, outside lid rough, inside lid, base, outside fine-finish, and finally painting. There is no reason why you can't modify the project and use a three-jaw chuck, a multi-chuck, or whatever, and revise the order accordingly.

Best to study the fabrication stages and then—in the light of your skill level and lathe equipment—adjust the techniques to suit you. However, before you do make firm decisions about size and method, be sure to visit a toy museum and a craft shop (a shop that sells craft items from Eastern Europe) and examine and handle as many different nest dolls as possible. Finally,

Fig. 19-2. Painting grid. By varying the painted imagery it is possible to achieve many traditional and nontraditional doll types.

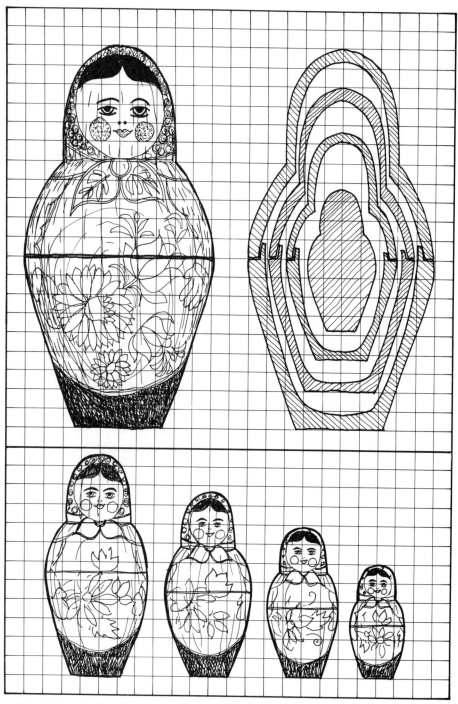

Fig. 19-3. Working drawing. (top) The scale is four grid squares to 1 inch.
Note in the section how the dolls are a loose fit one within another.

sit down with a pencil, ruler, paper, and colors, and draw your designs up to size.

TOOLS AND MATERIALS

You need ✦ Four lengths of easy-to-turn wood: one piece at 3 inches × 3 inches square and 6½ inches long for the largest doll; a piece at 2¼ inches × 2¼ inches square and 5½ inches long for the second from largest figure; a piece at 2 inches × 2 inches square and 4½ inches long for the second from smallest, and finally a piece at 1½ inches × 1½ inches square and 2½ inches long for the tiddler ✦ Workout paper ✦ Pencils and ruler ✦ Tracing paper ✦ Template card ✦ Scissors ✦ A rasp or plane ✦ The use of a small lathe ✦ A wood-screw chuck ✦ A good selection of wood-turning tools ✦ A pair of calipers ✦ A small straight saw ✦ A pack of graded sandpapers ✦ A selection of broad- and fine-point brushes ✦ Varnish ✦ A selection of acrylic paints, colors to suit ✦ The usual workshop items like cloths, paint tubs, water, and newpaper

DESIGNING AND CUTTING THE TEMPLATES

Finalize your designs to establish a good master profile; decide how many dolls you want in the nest. Draw the whole set of dolls out to size and work out the various cross sections and details.

Draw out the inside and outside profiles of each doll. Remember that wood thicknesses need to be turned down to about the ¼-inch mark and remember that all the figures must relate to each other in form and style.

Note the rim step or rebate detail and see how the dolls are a loose fit one within another. When you have achieved the profiles, take tracings, and

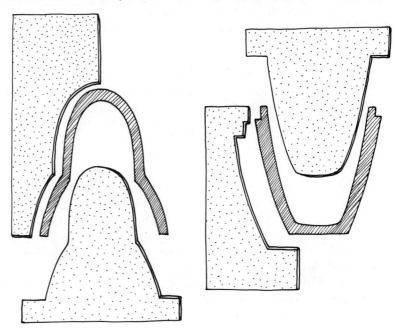

Fig. 19-4. Designing and cutting the templates. You need four separate templates for each doll.

carefully pencil-press transfer the traced lines through to the working face of the template card.

You need four templates for each doll: one for the outside head and shoulders profile; one for inside the lid; one for inside the base; and one for the outside base profile (FIG. 19-4). Make sure that all the templates relate correctly to each other and cut them out. Group the templates in sets and label them so that you don't have any mix-ups.

FIRST STEPS

Start with the largest doll. Take the 3-inch- × -3-inch square length of wood and prepare it for turning. Draw diagonals on the square cut ends, inscribe 2½-inch-diameter-circles, clear away the waste and mount it on the wood-screw chuck. (See other turned projects for pre-lathe safety checks).

With the dead center brought up to support the wood, swiftly turn it down to a clean 2½-inch-diameter cylinder. Draw the dead center back out of the way, reposition the tool rest over the lathe bed, and carefully true up the end-face of the cylinder.

With pencil, ruler, templates, and the parting tool, work from right to left along the work to establish: the length of the lid from the rim to the top of the head; the width of the base rebate; and the distance from the rebate down to the foot. If all is correct, you should be left with about 1¼ inches of waste at the screw chuck end of the work.

Mark off the various distances and use the parting tool to cut the ¼-inch-wide rebate to a depth of about ³⁄₁₆ inch. Take the calipers, the outside lid template, and the tools of your choice, and turn down the outside shape of the lid. Work from right to left to establish the curve of the belly and the shoulders, and the sharp angle at the neck.

Don't attempt to take the work to a smooth finish. Just settle for shaping the lid from the rim to the neck.

CUTTING THE LID

Note that the diameter of the wood across the rebate is now about 2⅛ inches. Position the tool rest at the end of the work and turn out the lid hollow. Be careful, don't jab the tool into the wood in an effort to quickly clear away the waste; start the cut with the parting tool or the point of the skew chisel to a depth of ¼ inch, and then hollow out the waste to that depth (FIG. 19-5, top).

Continue carefully, stepping deeper and deeper into the wood, until you reach the target depth. Remember that as you cut further and further into the hollow, you will have to keep moving the arm of the tool rest so that the edge of the tool is always supported as close as possible to the wood being worked. Get the arm of the rest as far as possible into the hollow and cut slowly and carefully.

Finally, finish the outside of the head, check the inside-lid profile against the template, and make sure that the lid fits the base rebate. Turn the outside of the lid to a good smooth finish and part off (FIG. 19-5, bottom).

CUTTING THE BASE

When you have parted off the lid, trim the face of the remaining cylinder and tidy up the rebate over which the lid will fit. Work the wood with a cautious little-by-little approach, all the while aiming for a tight friction fit of lid to base.

When you have cleared away most of the outside waste (the waste wood from the rim down to the foot) re-position the tool rest as close as possible to the end of the cylinder and start hollowing out the base (FIG. 19-6). Continue turning down the waste and stopping the lathe to make caliper and template checks.

When you have finished the base hollow, fit the lid and carefully turn the lid-to-base area down until the outside profile runs in a smooth uninterrupted curve from the shoulders to the foot. Remove the lid, finish cutting the foot and part off. Work the three largest dolls in like manner.

Note: the smallest doll (the solid doll) needs to be turned between centers.

PAINTING AND FINISHING

Clear away all the debris, make sure that the four dolls are free from dust, and move the work to the area that you have set aside for painting. Set the hollow turnings rim-side down, stand the solid doll on its base (best to have them on a rack) and apply a single thin coat of varnish. Don't labor over this stage, just settle for a swift, well-brushed, smooth, drip-free coat.

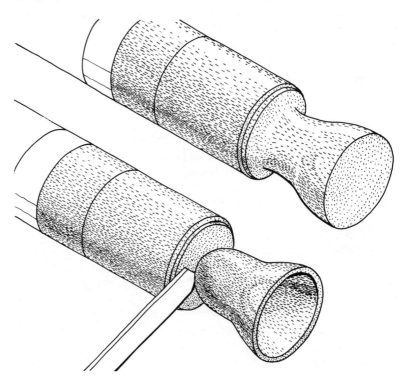

Fig. 19-5. Cutting the lid. (top) Rough out the basic cylinder and outside-lid form. (bottom) Hollow out the lid and complete the head.

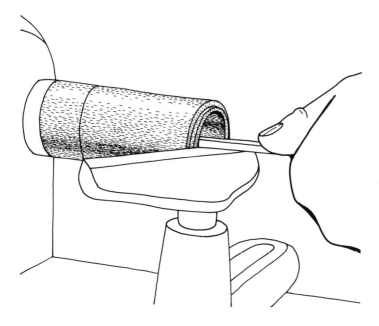

Fig. 19-6. Cutting the base. Hollow out the base and finish the base exterior.

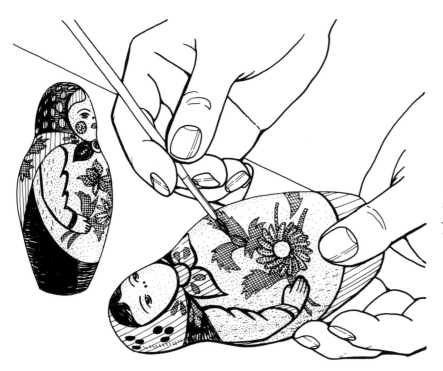

Fig. 19-7. Painting. Lay on the large blocks of ground color and use a fine-point brush to pick out the details.

While the varnish is drying, refresh your eyes by having a look at the project illustrations and the designs. Note the naive designs, the direct brush strokes and the swift, bold imagery, then take your brush and paint and have a practice run on some scrap wood.

When your wrists have loosened up, set to work on the figures. Block in the main areas of solid color (the heads and the feet), pick out the flowers with a swift series of on-and-off brush daubs, line in the edges, hair eyes, and face, and so on (FIG. 19-7).

Finally, when you have added all the little details and signed and dated the bottoms, lay on another coat of varnish and the job is done.

HINTS

If you like the idea of the project but consider the lids too difficult, you might modify the designs and work the nest of figures as a series of deep upside-down bowls that drop over each other.

It is most important that you choose your wood with care. Best to use a smooth-grained, knot-free wood like lime, sycamore, or plum.

Expect a certain amount of shrinkage as the wood dries out; allow for this when you fit the lid to the base.

If you decide to use a different lathe chuck and modify the order of working, make sure that the tops and bottoms of each doll are cut from the same piece of wood. If you make a doll from two different pieces of wood, you will have problems with shrinkage and fit.

If you want to clear the waste from the hollows with a drill, see other turned projects.

Traditionally most dolls are decorated to show off the wood grain; leave the interiors plain.

Some designs have a broad spreading flare or foot on the largest doll.

Making an
American Stick Doll

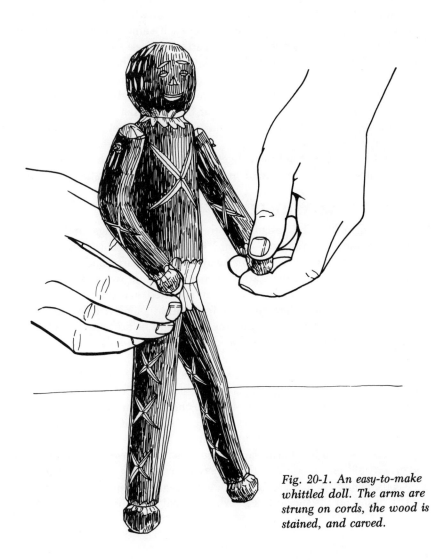

Fig. 20-1. An easy-to-make
whittled doll. The arms are
strung on cords, the wood is
stained, and carved.

STICK DOLLS—KNOWN VARIOUSLY AROUND THE WORLD AS PEGS DOLLS, GER-man figures, Italian dolls, Dutch or Deutsch dolls, and American stick dolls—are characterized by being made of "found" wood, by being turned, carved or whittled, and by having movable joints. Stick dolls are made in just about every rural and ethnic country that you care to think of, and belong to the peasant toy making tradition.

In Europe, stick and Dutch dolls—worked as part of a cottage industry—were traditionally whittled and carved in the winter, sold to traveling buyers, sold by the middle men to stores, shops, and exporters, and finally sold in various sizes and sets to the doll buying public.

Because some of the more expensive dolls had hinged knees, hips, shoulders, and elbows, they didn't really belong to any definite style or type. They simply drew their inspiration directly from the availability of certain tools and materials and from the environment in which they were made.

And so it was that when many of these self same European peasants decided to build a new life in the American wilderness, they took their toy and doll making traditions with them. This being so, when some poor care-worn German-American settler was nagged by his daughters into making a doll, he didn't consciously consider how the doll ought to be styled; but rather, just as his father and grandfather had done before him, he looked to available tools and materials, and related to quiet echoes of half-remembered traditions.

Then, as now, by the time a likely looking Y-shaped crutch has been cut and knife-honed to a razor sharpness, the doll is more than halfway made.

CONSIDERING THE PROJECT

Have a good look at the designs and the working drawings, and see how the doll is made from an upside down Y crutch (FIGS. 20-1 through 20-3).

Note how the bark has been cut away, the white sap wood stained, and the features cut through the stain to reveal the white wood beneath.

The shoulders and arms are pierced and pivoted on a knotted cord. With a doll of this type and character, the fabrication stages are so basic, and the wood so easily found, that really the doll might be described as a throw-away. Meaning that because the doll can easily be made from stick wood, if it gets lost or broken, another can soon be made.

I've got the feeling that—rather like the making of whittled whistles, linked chains and ball-in-cage tricks—making of stick dolls was one of those "made-on-the-porch" party pieces to keep the kids amused.

So there you have it, if you have a sharp clasp knife, a good source of green off-the-tree stick wood, a dark staining pigment, a length or two of twine, and an awl or hand drill—and if you want to win over all your children and grandchildren—then this is the project for you. Imagine, a knife, a piece of sweet-smelling apple wood, and an hour or two spent in front of a blazing log fire or out on the sun lounger—what a great way to spend an evening.

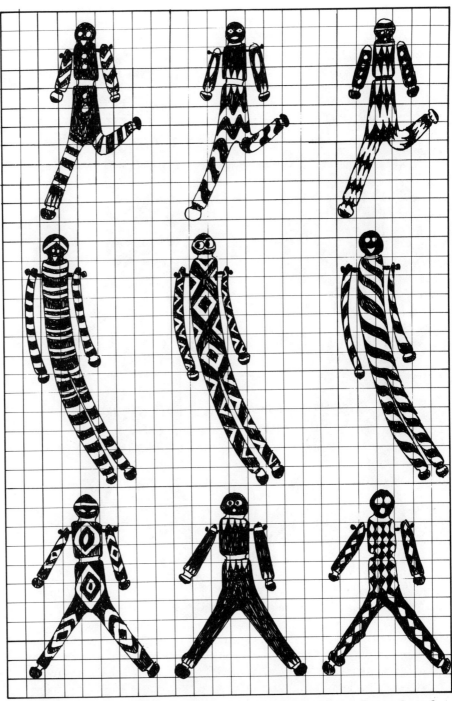

Fig. 20-2. Painting grid. By searching around for interesting forked sticks and by working various painted patterns, it is possible to create many novel doll forms.

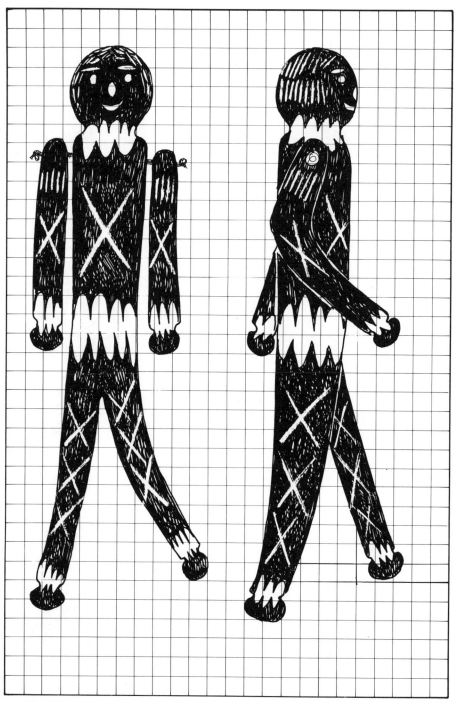

Fig. 20-3. Working drawings. At a scale of four grid squares to 1 inch, the dolls stand about 7 to 8 inches high. You can, of course, make a much larger or a much smaller doll.

TOOLS AND MATERIALS

You need ✦ A hand-sized Y crutch with arms about 5 inches long, and a handle section about 1½ inches long ✦ A sharp knife ✦ A fine-point scalpel ✦ A hand drill with a ⅛-inch-diameter drill bit ✦ About 6 inches of strong twine ✦ A permanent felt-tip marker, it could be black or colored ✦ A dab of furniture wax

FIRST STEPS

Cut a catapult type Y-shaped crutch that measures about 5 inches long from the central fork to the ends of the head and foot extremities. Take a sharp knife and skin away all the bark and bumps; work toward a smooth fork-to-head thickness of 1¼ inches, and a leg thickness of around ½ inch. Measure off 2½ inches along the legs, and cut off the two arm pieces at 2½ inches (FIG. 20-4).

You should have three pieces of wood: the main body-to-foot crutch and the two arms. Spend time with the knife bringing the wood to a good finish. Aim for ends that are nicely rounded and smooth.

SHAPING

Have a look at the working drawings and see how the wood has been wasted at the neck, wrists, and ankles; nothing fancy just a swift cutting away with the knife.

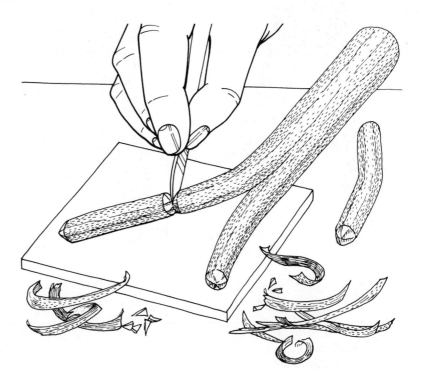

Fig. 20-4. First steps. Measure off about 2½ inches from the fork and cut off two arm pieces at 2½ inches long.

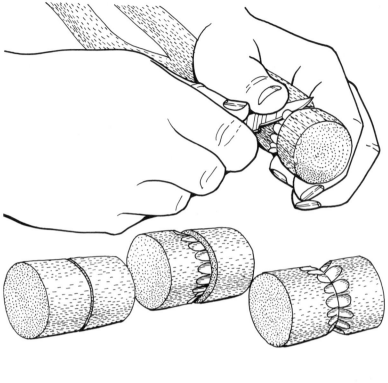

Fig. 20-5. Shaping. (top) Run the knife, at an angle, into the initial stop-cut and work a V section neck. (bottom from left to right) To cut a "neck", trim off the bark and make a stop-cut around the wood, make angled paring cuts to one side of the stop-cut, make angled cuts into the side of the stop-cuts, and remove the waste.

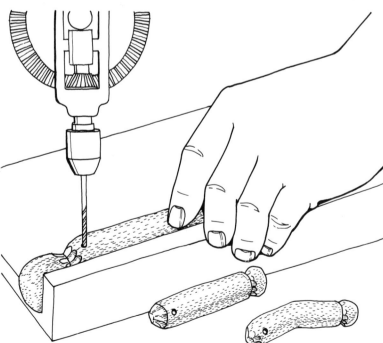

Fig. 20-6. Drill ⅛-inch-diameter holes through the arms and the shoulders and string up.

Start with the neck, and run the point of the knife around and into the wood to a depth of about ⅛ inch for a clean well established stopcut. With the crutch held firmly in one hand and the knife in the other—and with the stopcut living up to its name—run the knife at an angle down into the wood toward the base of the stopcut to remove small chips or wedges (FIG. 20-5).

Work around the wood on either side of the stopcut to achieve a V-shaped scoop or trench. Continue at the neck, wrists, and ankles. Finally, swiftly run the knife over the wood so that all the shapes run smoothly into each other.

DRILLING, STAINING, AND DECORATING

When you have worked all the "necked" whittlings, take the drill and the ⅛-inch-diameter drill bit and—with a friend to hold the wood—work pivotal holes through the top of the arms and through the shoulders (FIG. 20-6).

Use the black felt-tip marker, or use ink, lamp black, acrylic paint, or berry juice, and stain and cover all the white wood.

When the stain is dry, have a last look at all the inspirational designs, then take the knife and the scalpel and cut in all the incised patterns, motifs, and details of your chosen doll (FIG. 20-2). Meaning, as with the "necks," make a series of stopcuts and angled cuts to achieve V-section incisions. Don't cut too deep, just aim to cut away the stained skin to reveal the white wood beneath.

FIXING THE PIVOTAL CORD, AND FINISHING

When all the decorative details have been swiftly cut in, knot the end of the cord, thread the arms to the body, draw another knot tight up against the work, and trim off. Finally, burnish the whole project with a dab of furniture wax and a soft cloth and the job is done.

HINTS

If you like the idea of the project, but want to go for a more exciting form, search out interesting bent and contorted roots and branches. Best go for easy-to-carve woods like juniper roots, and plum and apple trimmings.

If you want to make a more complex project, make a doll with movable joints at the neck, shoulder, elbows, hips, knees, and ankles.

Index

wood (see also lumber), 10
  apple, 1
  ash, 1
  beech, 1
  boxwood, 1
  cherry, 2
  exotic, 4
  faults in, 1, 14
  filler for, 9
  holly, 6
  lime, 8
  maple, 8
  parana pine, 9
  pine, 9
  plum, 10

plywood, 10
prepared, 10
rosewood, 10
sycamore, 13
wood-screw chuck, 105
wood-turning tools, 15
woodscrew chuck, 15
work-out paper, 15
workbench, 15
working drawings, 15
working face, 15

Y

yo-yo, 17-26

Other Bestsellers From TAB

☐ **MARIONETTE MAGIC: FROM CONCEPT TO CURTAIN CALL**—Bruce Taylor, Illustrations by Cathy Stubington and Bruce Taylor

Puppets are fun weekend projects and offer a welcomechallenge to the woodworker who is seeking a change of pace. Requiring no prior puppet-making experience, this book provides a complete apprenticeship in puppet-making, as well as a concise course in staging. Taylor describes how you can transform wood, plaster, and papier-mache into animated figures. Complete plans and detailed instructions are accompanied by tips and tricks of the trade. 176 pp., 143 illus., 7″ × 10″
Paper $15.95   **Hard $19.95**
Book No. 3091

☐ **DESIGNING AND BUILDING SPACE-SAVING FURNITURE, WITH 28 PROJECTS**—2nd Edition—Percy W. Blandford

Step-by-step directions, exploded diagrams and two-color illustrations are included with detailed advice on planning and preparing, measuring, woodworking techniques, fasteners, upholstery, and tool usage. Author Percy Blandford is an internationally recognized master craftsman. He has been writing about the how-tos of woodworking since 1940. In this book, he provides a wealth of easy-to-accomplish projects for increasing storage space in every room in your home. 192 pp., 200 illus., 2-color throughout
Paper $17.95   **Hard $21.95**
Book No. 3074

☐ **DESIGNING AND BUILDING CHILDRENS' FURNITURE, WITH 61 PROJECTS**—2nd Edition—Percy W. Blandford

This book provides complete detail in measuring, marking, designing, building, and finishing child-size furniture. Projects include a baby's playpen, chest of drawers, safety gate, toy box, painting easel, rocking horse, and more. Percy W. Blandford is a recognized authority in woodworking and other practical crafts. His superb line drawings illustrate this step-by-step guide. 192 pp., Over 150 illus.
Paper $17.95   **Hard $21.95**
Book No. 3064

☐ **101 OUTSTANDING WOODEN TOYS AND CHILDRENS' FURNITURE PROJECTS**—Wayne L. Kadar

Turn inexpensive materials into fun and functional toys. Challenge and charm the youngsters in your life with building blocks, pull toys, shape puzzles, stilts, trains, trucks, boats, planes, dolls and more. This step-by-step guide is abundantly illustrated and provides complete materials lists. 304 pp., 329 illus.
Paper $19.95   **Hard $24.95**
Book No. 3058

☐ **BUILD YOUR OWN GRANDFATHER CLOCK AND SAVE**—John A. Nelson

Thorough and exact plans make this challenging project achievable by woodworkers of all skill levels. The design is an adaptation of two or three clocks made by 18th-century clockmaker Nathaniel Mulliken. Every aspect of construction is covered, from building the case and hood to installing pre-made movements. Nelson even details how to make your own brass hinges and escutcheons from scratch. Many illustrations complement the step-by-step instructions. 144 pp., 99 illus.
Paper $15.95   **Hard $19.95**
Book No. 3053

☐ **WOODWORKER'S 30 BEST PROJECTS**—Editors of *Woodworker* Magazine

A collection of some of the finest furniture ever made can be found within the pages of this project book. Designed for the woodworker who has already mastered the basics, the projects presented in this book are for the intermediate- to advanced-level craftsman. Each furniture project comes complete with detailed instructions, a materials list, exploded views of working diagrams, a series of step-by-step, black-and-white photos, and a photograph of the finished piece. 224 pp., 300 illus.
Paper $18.95   **Hard $23.95**
Book No. 3021

Other Bestsellers From TAB

☐ **20 INNOVATIVE ELECTRONICS PROJECTS FOR YOUR HOME**—Joseph O'Connell

O'Connell carefully guides the budding inventory and enhances the ability of the experienced designer. This book is a no-nonsense approach to building unusual yet practical electronic devices. More than just a collection of 20 projects, this book provides helpful hints and sound advice for the experimenter and home hobbyist. Particular emphasis is placed on unique yet truly useful devices that are justifiably time- and cost-efficient. Projects include a protected outlet box (for your computer system) . . . a variable ac power controller . . . a remote volume control . . . a fluorescent bike light . . . and a pair of active minispeakers with built-in amplifiers. 256 pp., 130 illus.

Paper $17.50   **Hard $21.95**
Book No. 2947

☐ **COUNTRY FURNITURE**—114 Traditional Projects—Percy W. Blandford

Show off a house full of beautiful country furniture—you created! There is an undeniable attraction about handmade furniture. Whether the craftsman is an amateur or professional, individually made furniture carries on the tradition of the first settlers and their ancestors. Blandford captures the rustic flavor in these traditional projects—and shows how you can too! Projects range from simple boxes to more elaborate cabinets and cupboards. 260 pp., 246 illus.

Paper $19.95   **Had $24.95**
Book No. 2944

☐ **FRAMES AND FRAMING: THE ULTIMATE ILLUSTRATED HOW-TO-DO-IT GUIDE**—Gerald F. Laird and Louise Meière Dunn, CPF

This illustrated step-by-step guide gives complete instructions and helpful illustrations on how to cut mats, choose materials, and achieve attractively framed art. Filled with photographs and eight pages of full color, this book shows why a frame's purpose is to enhance, support, and protect the artwork, and never call attention to itself. You can learn how to make a beautiful frame that complements artwork. 208 pp., 264 illus., 8 pages full color

Paper $15.95   **Hard $19.95**
Book No. 2909

☐ **YEAR-ROUND CRAFTS FOR KIDS**—Barbara L. Dondiego, Illustrated by Jacqueline Cawley

Easy to use, the handy month-by-month format provides a year of inspiring projects, many focused on seasonal themes to ensure young children's enthusiasm. Valentines, paper airplanes, and cookies for Easter, paper bag bunny puppets, string painting, Hanukkah candles and gingerbread boys, bell and candle mobiles and of course Christmas trees for December are just a few of the fun things to make. 256 pp., 180 illus., plus 8 pages of color

Paper $15.95   **Hard $19.95**
Book No. 2904

☐ **BUILD YOUR OWN WORKING FIBEROPTIC, INFRARED AND LASER SPACE-AGE PROJECTS**—Robert E. Iannini

Here are plans for a variety of useful electronic and scientific devices, including a high sensitivity laser light detector and a high voltage laboratory generator (useful in all sorts of laser, plasma ion, and particle applications as well as for lighting displays and special effects). And that's just the beginning of the exciting space age technology that you'll be able to put to work! 288 pp., 198 illus.

Paper $18.95   **Hard $24.95**
Book No. 2724

☐ **BUILDING METAL LOCATORS: A Treasure Hunter's Project Book**—Charles D. Rakes

If you've dreamed of discovering a buried treasure—stop dreaming and open this guide packed with everything you need to get started building an exciting, low-cost alternative to expensive commercially made metal locators. The detectors included here will locate anything from coins and jewelry to gold and silver and can be built by any electronics enthusiast with the ability to follow schematic diagrams. 126 pp., 102 illus.

Paper $12.95   **Hard $15.95**
Book No. 2706

☐ **A MASTER CARVER'S LEGACY**—essentials of wood carving techniques—Brieuc Bouché

Expert guidance on the basics of wood carving from a master craftsman with over 50 years experience. All the techniques for making a whole range of woodcarved items are included. You'll learn how-to's for basic chip carving, the basic rose, cutting of twinings, a classic acanthus leaf, and a simple carving in the round. In no time at all you will be making many of the projects featured. 176 pp., 135 illus., 8 1/2" × 11"

Paper $17.95   **Hard $24.95**
Book No. 2629

Other Bestsellers From TAB